Burt Franklin: Research and Source Works Series # 69

MACHIAVELLI

AND THE

ELIZABETHAN DRAMA.

MACHIAVELLI

AND THE

ELIZABETHAN DRAMA,

VON

EDWARD MEYER.

Burt Franklin: Research and Source Works Series # 69

**BURT FRANKLIN
NEW YORK**

Published by

BURT FRANKLIN
514 West 113th Street
New York 25, N. Y.

ORIGINALLY PUBLISHED
WEIMAR - 1897
LITTERARHISTORISCHE FORSCHUNGREN

To My Father

In Love and Gratitude.

Errata.

Owing to the author's absence in America during the printing of this work, various mistakes have been left standing, of which the principal are:

P. 2, l. 12: instead of *at* read *as*.

„ 5, Note 1, l. 5: instead of *excusabunt* read *excusabant*.

„ 5, Note 1, l. 11 read: non maxime arridere, eadem tamen si exerceret, se idem judicare, quod reliqui omnes, quicumque de Regis, vel Principis viri institutione scripserant, & experientia docet, breve ejus imperium futurum; id quod maxime exoptabat etc.

„ 19, l. 4: instead of *die* read *de*.

„ 19, Note 5, l. 3: instead of *Catab* read *Cantab*.

„ 19, Note 5, last l.: „ „ *loco* „ *locum*.

„ 22, line [25] read: Ingenij monumenta mei etc.

„ 22, l. 6 from bottom: instead of *us* read *as*.

„ 24, last line of text: „ „ *come* read *came*.

„ 25, l. 15 read: Lagicalia.

„ 31, l. 20 read: perhaps Iago in.

„ 41, Note 4, l 7: instead of *few* read *Jew*.

„ 47, l. 9 from bottom: instead of *her* read *his*.

Contents.

Preface.

One word by way of preface is necessary for the understanding of this dissertation. Four years ago when first making the acquaintance of Kyd, Marlowe, Greene, Peele, Jonson, Chapman, Marston, Dekker, Middleton, Webster, Massinger, Ford, and other of Shakspere's great contemporaries, I was struck by the number of times Machiavelli and Aretino were referred to, and the reckless manner in which, what I then supposed to be the former's political principles, were cited and put into practice by the villains of dramatic literature. Having determined to investigate to what extent this had been done, a careful study was first made of Machiavelli: then the drama was reread. To my surprise, I found that what the Elizabethans reverted to so often as the maxims of the Florentine statesman, were, in four cases out of five, not to be found in his writings at all; but were perverted from the same in a manner infinitely unjust. The natural conclusion was, that they could not have been taken directly from the works of the great politician. This was strengthened by the fact that, (with the exception of the "Arte della Guerra", a work of minor import, translated by Whitehorne in 1560/62, 1573/74, 1588, and the "Storia Fiorentina", translated by Bedingfield in 1595) the weightiest writings of Machiavelli remained un-Englished till Dacre's version of the "Discorsi" in 1636 and of the "Principe" in 1640: i. e. his real political axioms

were not given to the English public in its own language
until half a century after the dramatists were making, or
rather, thought they were making, such prodigal use of
the same.

While ransacking the British Museum for more light
on the subject, I came across Gentillet's "Discours sur les
Moyens de bien gouverner et maintenir en bonne paix un
Royaume ou autre Principauté . . . Contre Nicholas Machiavel,
Florentin, 1576", popularly called "Contre-Machiavel", which,
as students know from Mohl ("Geschichte und Literatur der
Staatswissenschaften"), and Villari ("Niccolò Machiavelli e
i suoi tempi"), was wide read and used by the Florentine's
antagonists during the 16th and 17th centuries. Scarcely
were a few pages perused, when it became perfectly evident,
that this was the book from which the dramatists drew: a
careful study of the same, together with the discovery that
an English translation was made by one Simon Patericke
in 1577, the year after its appearance in French, has proved
Gentillet, beyond a doubt, the source of all the Elizabethan
misunderstanding.

Dr. Grosart, in his edition of Quarles (III, 334), remarks: "It were one of the "Curiosities of Literature" to
bring together the many early references in our literature
to the famous Italian, Machiavelli (and so Mahomet)." He
might have added Aretino, more often cited and calumniated
than the other two combined. The same erudite scholar
notes in his "Poems of Marston" (243): "I have suggested
to the biographer of the renowned Machiavelli (Professor
Villari of Florence) that an odd chapter might be written
on the *scare* that his name was for long in England: so
much so that he came to be regarded as an incarnation of
the Evil One himself. Probably such chapter will be written."
Such, however, was never composed for reasons which
Dr. Grosart kindly imparted to me in a letter, dated "Bank
Villa, Dublin. 18th Sept. 1895.": "Eheu! Just before my
utter break-down from overwork I had drawn up a list of

(I think) 310 references in old English literature to Machiavelli, intending to forward it to Prof. Villari as a contri-
bution to his great life of Machiavelli. But unluckily in
clearing out the chaos of my papers this elaborate list must
have got into the waste-paper basket or flames: for it has
never turned up. For two years I was almost completely
laid aside, and so the matter passed from my memory. It was
a singularly curious list, and your letter renews the pang
of its loss."

During the course of reading I have noted no less than
395 references to Machiavelli in Elizabethan literature, (and
over 500 to Aretino which I hope to incorporate in the
near future). To publish these alone would, indeed, be to
make an unique addition to Disraeli; it seemed more advisable, however, to arrange them in chronological order as far
as possible, and use the citations in popular literature as a
foil to those in the drama, omitting such as were mere
mentions of the name, or had no contingency with "the
bugbear of the stage" and its villainy. As in most works
dealing with the period under discussion, this thesis treats
mainly of the acted drama, though the book-drama is
occasionly adverted to where apposite. Absolutely no pre-
tension has been made to literary style; the facts having
been expressed as baldly and succinctly as possible. The
utmost conservatism has been used throughout, for as Burd
has shown, but few of Machiavelli's renowned maxims ori-
ginate strictly with him: they were more the result of his
classic reading. Thus, to take e. g. the principle, most used
by the dramatists:

Machiavelli says:

"Essendo adunque un principe necessitato sapere bene
usare la bestia, debbe di quella pigliare la volpe ed
il leone; perchè il lione non si difende dai lacci, la
volpe non si difende da' lupi. Bisogna adunque essere
volpe a conoscere i lacci, e lione a sbigottire i lupi."
Prin. 18.

Plutarch said:

τῶν δ᾽ ἀξιούντων μὴ πολεμεῖν μετὰ δόλου τοὺς ἀφ᾽ Ἡρακλέους
γεγονότας καταγελᾶν ἐκέλευε· ὅπου γὰρ ἡ λεοντῆ μὴ ἐφικνεῖται,
προσραπτέον ἐκεῖ τὴν ἀλωπεκῆν.   Lysander VII.

Cicero said:

"Quum autem duobus modis, id est, aut vi aut fraude,
fiat injuria; fraus quasi vulpeculae, vis leonis videtur;
utrumque homine alienissimum; sed fraus odio digna
majore. Totius autem injustitiae nulla capitalior est,
quam eorum, qui, quum maxime fallunt, id agunt, ut
viri boni videantur." De. Off. I, 13.

and the probable source in the end is Pindar:

τόλμᾳ γὰρ εἰκώς
θυμὸν ἐριβρεμετᾶν θηρῶν λεόντων
ἐν πόνῳ· μῆτιν δ᾽ ἀλώπηξ, αἰετοῦ ἅτ᾽ ἀναπιτναμένα ῥόμβον ἴσχει.
χρὴ δὲ πᾶν ἔρδοντ᾽ ἀμαυρῶσαι τὸν ἐχθρόν.   Isth. Odes 3, 63 sqq.

Greene acknowledged Plutarch as his source in "Selimus";
Jonson refers often enough to Cicero and Pindar.

I would here most respectfully beg the honor of ex-
pressing my sincere gratitude to Prof. Dr. Schick, Prof.
Dr. Braune and Prof. Dr. Neumann of the "Grofsherzogliche
Ruprecht-Karls-Universität" in Heidelberg, and to Prof.
Dr. Sievers, Prof. Dr. Wülker, and Prof. Dr. von Bahder
of the "Königliche Sächsische Universität" in Leipzig, for
the guidance of my University studies

Introduction.*⁾

The Source of Machiavellianism in the Elizabethan Drama.

> "Truely the world has had a pother with this
> little Niccolò Macchiavelli and his perverse
> little Book." Carlyle: "Fred. II."

All students of Elizabethan literature must have observed, that to most authors of this period, Machiavelli appeared as the very devil incarnate, or, at least, as the incorporation of all hypocrisy. To understand the peculiar light, the demoniac aureole, which palliated the true Machiavelli[1] from Marlowe, Shakspere, Jonson, Chapman, and their contemporaries, it is essential to cast a bird's-eye view over the reception, accorded to the great politician's work (*Il Principe*) from his own day to that of Elizabeth. The "Principe" is the book by which the Florentine is best known; and it

---

*) This chapter is based upon the researches of Nitti: "Machiavelli nella vita e nelle opere", Villari: "Niccolò Machiavelli e i suoi tempi", Leo: "Studien und Skizzen zu einer Naturlehre des Staates", Burd: „Il Principe", Mohl: "Die Geschichte und Literatur der Staatswissenschaften", Janet: "Histoire de la science politique dans ses rapports avec la morale", and others less important.

[1] Cf. Ward: "— that old bugbear of English theatrical audiences, Macchiavelli, who is the villain proper of the pièce" [Lee's "Caesar Borgia"] Hist. Dram. Poet. II, 545. —

Cf. Grosart: "Hall's Poems" (231) "Machiavelli came in vulgar speech and belief to typify the Devil".

Meyer, Machiavelli.

has called forth almost all the comment. Since it contained the very gist of all Machiavelli's political writings, and, as will be seen, was the source (at second-hand) of all the Elizabethan "scare", that work, alone, calls for consideration in the present discussion.

The "Principe" was planned in April[1]) and completed[2]) in December[3]) 1513. It remained in MS. until five years after the author's death, but was, never-the-less, widely read. In 1523, Nifo deliberately pirated[4]) the whole treatise, translated it into Latin with interpolations, and published it as his own,[5]) adding a chapter of "antidote to the poison": which method as will be shown, was much followed by French and English writers in the time of Elizabeth and later on.

Clement VII decreed,[6]) Aug. 23. 1531, the publication of Machiavelli's works; in 1532 appeared two editions of the "Principe"; one by Blado, the other by Giunta.[7]) In the following eighteen years there were no less than twenty-three editions in Italian. The first English translation of which there is a copy extant appeared in 1640.[8]) The

---

[1]) Mach. Op. VIII, 36: Letter to Vettori. (The edition used throughout is the "Italia" 1813.)

[2]) Leo has no authority for the statement that the last chapter was an afterthought for Lorenzo de' Medici. Cf. "Studien und Skizzen" p. 36.

[3]) Mach. Op. VIII, 96: Letter to Vettori.

[4]) Nourisson, Mach. 1883, ch. 12—14.

[5]) Augustini Niphi Medicae philosophi suessoni de regnandi peritia ad Carolum V Imper. Caesarem semper Augustum. Neapoli 1523.

Cf. Burd: "Il Prin." p. 44.

[6]) Papal bull in Amico: La Vita di Nic. Mach. 1876, p. 415.

[7]) Blado's ed. contains "Il Principe", "Ritratti delle cose della Francia" and "Ritratti delle cose della Alamagna": Giunta's, these three together with "Vita di Castruccio Castracani" and "Il Modo che tenne il Duca Valentino nello ammazzare Vitellozzo Vitelli".

[8]) "Nicholas Machiavel's Prince also the Life of Castruccio Castracani of Lucca and the means Duke Valentine us'd to put to death Vitelozzo

Elizabethan play-wrights had the "Prince" always within easy reach, however, in the French translation of 1553; [1]) and in that of 1586, [2]) which appeared just when the great drama was burgeoning. To scholars it was known by the Latin translations of 1560, 1566, 1581, 1589, 1594, 1599, 1622, 1648 etc. etc. There may have been an English edition, now lost, earlier than that of 1640; for this most widely read of all Machiavelli's works would hardly have remained unenglished, when less important works, such as "The Arte of Warre", [3]) and "The Florentine Historie", [4]) had been published. The "Discourses" [5]) and Belphegor [6]) appeared much later.

The "Principe", even in the year after its composition, must have called forth comment, if not denunciation; for Buonaccorsi mentions such [7]) in a letter to Pandolfus Bellacio.

Vitelli, Oliverotto of Fermo, Paul, and the Duke of Gravina. Translated out of Italian by E[dward] D[acres]." pp. 305. London 1640. 12⁰.

The "Prince" appeared again with the "Discourses" in 1663—61: 2nd ed. 1674.

[1]) "Le Prince . . . . Traduit d'Italien en Françoys par G. Cappel. Paris 1553."

[2]) „Les Discours . . . . Ensemble un livre du mesme auteur intitulé le Prince." Rouen 1586.

[3]) "The Arte of Warre . . . . Set forthe in Englishe by P. Whitehorne. 1560—62, 1573—74, 1588."

[4]) "The Florentine Historie . . . . Translated into English by T[homas] B[edinfield] Esquire 1595."

[5]) The "Discourses" were translated very shortly before "The Prince" by the same author: „Machiavel's Discourses . . . . with some marginal animadversions by E[dward] D[acres] 1636. All translations after 1666 are beyond the discussion; of importance, however, are "Flor. Hist." by M. R. 1674. "Complete Works" by [Henry Nevile] 1675, 1680, 1694, 1720: by Farneworth 1762, 1775.

[6]) "The Devil a Married Man" [Machiavelli's Belphegor] 1647. Brit. Mus. [Cat.]

[7]) "Ti mando l'operetta, composta, nuovamente de' Principati dal nostro Niccolò Machiavelli nella quale tu troverai con 'somma dilucidatà e brevità descritte tutte le qualità de' Principati . . . . Ricevilo adunque con quella prontezza che si ricerca, e preparati acerrimo difensore contro

Vettori, like Machiavelli a profound thinker, expressed the
delight which it gave to politicians.[1]) Guicciardini, as is
well known, praised the work highly. It was, however,
resented by many; and Bussini did not hesitate to ascribe
to it the refusal of the "Ten" to receive Machiavelli[2]) into
service again at the enfranchisement of Florence in 1527.
Up to 1532, there is no evidence that the *prima facie* in-
tention of the book was doubted; but in that year, Giunta
prefixed to his edition a letter broaching the *double entendre*
view,[3]) which was to become so popular.

Farneworth[4]) thought, that the idea of the "Prince" a
satire originated with Gentilis; but many years before the latter's
"De Legatibus", Cardinal Pole published, in 1535, his "De

a tutti quelli, che per malignità o invidia lo volessino, secondo l'uso
di questi tempi, mordere e lacerare." Mach. Op. I, XLII. This was
written in 1514. Polidori: Arch. St. Ital., vol. IV pt. 2. Cf. also Burd,
op. cit. 34.

[1]) Ho visto e' capitoli dell' Opera vostra, e mi piacciono oltre a
modo.   Vettori to Mach. June 15, 1514.

[2]) "Cerco con grande instanza di entrare nel suo luogo dei Dieci,
Zanobi e Luigi lo favorivano assai, ma M. Baldassari, e Niccolò di
Braccio lo disfavorivano: e l'universale per conto del suo Principe; ai
ricchi pareva che quel Principe fosse stato un documento da insegnare
al Duca tor loro tutta la roba, e a' poveri tutta la libertà. Ai Piagnoni
pareva che e' fosse eretico, ai buoni disonesto, ai tristi più tristo, o
valente di loro: talchè ognuno l'odiava."
               Bussini a Varchi. Jan. 23, 1549. Lett. di Gio. Buss. p. 75.

[3]) "Al Molto Reverendo Monsignore Messer Giovanni Gaddi ....
U. S. R. la quale (anchor che forse non ben degno de la sua grandezza)
lo pigliera nondimeno volentieri; et con quello animo, ch' io gliełlo
porgo; et lo difendera da quegli, che per il soggetto suo lo vanno tutto
il giorno lacerando si aspramente: non sapendo, che quegli, che l' herbe
et le medicine insegnano; insegnano parimente anchora i veleni; solo
accioche da quegli ci passiamo cognoscendogli guardare: ne s'accorgono
anco, che egli non è arte, ne scientia alcuna: la quale non si possa da
quegli, che cattivi sono, usare malamente: et chi dira mai, che il ferro
fusse trovato più tosto per ammazzare gli huomini, che per difendersi
da gli animali? Princ. ed. Giunta 1532 p. I.

[4]) Farnew. op. cit. I, 482.

Unitate Ecclesiae", which imputed this solution of the book's meaning to Machiavelli himself.[1]) Gentilis merely follows the Cardinal, but says nothing, relative to the source of the theory.[2]) Burd says: "it is impossible to call in question Pole's honesty"; but let any one read the great Cardinal's vile, dishonest defamation[3]) of Machiavelli dead, and then ask himself, if the integrity of a man, who could write thus, is to be relied upon when inspired by rabid antagonism.

That Matteo[4]) supported the same theory forty-three years later merely shows he was conversant with Pole's writings.

---

[1]) "At vero, quod ad Machiavellum attinet, si verum sit, quod Florentiae superiori hyeme cum eo in itinere divertissem, cum de occasione scribendi illum librum, tum de animi ejus in eodem proposito audivi, de hac caecitate et ignorantia aliqua ex parte excusari potest, ut eum tum excusabant cives ejus cum sermone introducto de illius libro hanc impiam caecitatem objecissem; ad quod illi responderunt idem, quod dicebant ab ipso Machiavello, 'cum idem illi aliquando opponeretur, fuisse responsum, se non solum quidem judicium suum in illo libro fuisse sequutum, sed illius ad quem scriberet, quem cum sciret tyrannica natura fuisse, ea inseruit, quae non potuerunt tali naturae non maxime exoptabat, cum intus odio flagraret illius Principis, ad quem scriberet; neque aliud spectasse in eo libro, quam scribendo ad tyrannum ea quae tyranno placent, eum sua sponte ruentem praecipitem, si posset, clare. Haec quidem illi, ut caecitatem mentis Machiavelli excusarent." Epis. Reg. Pole: 1744 p. 151.

[2]) "Sui propositi non est Tyrannum instruere, sed arcanis ejus palam factis, ipsum miseris populis nudum et conspicuum exhibere. An enim tales quales ipse describit Principes fuisse plurimos ignoramus!" Gent. De. Legat. lib. III, c. 9.

[3]) "Talem autem librum illum inveni scriptum ab hoste humani generis, in quo omnia hostis consilia explicantur, et modi quibus religio, pietas, et omnes virtutis indoles, facilius destrui possent. Liber enim etsi hominis nomen et stylum prae se ferat, tamen, vix coepi legere, quin Satanae digito scriptum agnoscerem .... omnem malitiam Satanae redolent. Inter reliqua vero librum de Principe fecit .... in quo talem nobis Principem exprimit qualem certe, si Satanas in carne regnaret, et filium haberet, quem post se in regno relicturus esset, cum carnem consummasset, non alia prorsus praecepta filio suo daret." Pole, op. cit. 136.

[4]) Peplus Ital. 1578. p. 52. Cf. Burd 38.

Thus the English Cardinal was the first to really proclaim the *double entendre* theory, broached by Giunta, and to denounce Machiavelli as in league with the devil: this is to be borne in mind, it being of singular significance for the Florentine's later reputation in England. In 1540, Varchi praised Machiavelli highly, but inveighed bitterly against the "Principe"; and made the absurd statement, which no one else has adopted, that the author sought to destroy this his best work.[1]) The progress of the reformation naturally called forth from the Romish church an attack upon all writings which questioned the infallibility of the Pope: Machiavelli had promulgated views entirely too emancipated, and could not escape condemnation. In 1550, Mazio denounced him to the Inquisition. Two years later, Ambrogio Caterino polemicised fiercely against the "Discorsi" and the "Principe", in his "De libris a christiano detestandis". [2]) This was followed in the same year by the rabid assault of the famous Ossorio. Two points in Machiavelli's writings were especially oppugned; the daring comparison of Christianity with Paganism (Discorsi II, 2), and the strictures upon Moses (Principe VI). In 1557, Paulus Jovius proclaimed him an illiterate atheist;[3]) and the Jesuits burned him in effigy[4]) at Ingolstadt. In the same year at Rome the Inquisition decreed the utter destruction

---

[1]) "Quell' opera (il Principe) .... empia veramente e da dover essere non solo biasimata, ma spenta, come cercò di fare egli stesso dopo il rivolgimento dello stato, non essendo ancora stampata." Stor. Fior. I, 210.

[2]) In the chapter "Quam execrandi Machiavelli Discursus et Institutis sui Principis."

[3]) He calls him "atheos" and says: "Nulla vel certe mediocris Latinarum literarum cognitio fuit." Paul. Jov. Elog. cap. 87.

[4]) Apponendovi questa inscrizione: "Quoniam fuit homo vafer ac subdolus, diabolicarum cogitationum faber optimus, cacodaemonis auxiliator." Ugo Foscolo: Prose letterarie 1850 vol. II p. 452. Villari II, 412.

of Machiavelli's works; [1]) and two years later the edict was published. The Council of Trent confirmed the index; and it was reissued in 1564. [2]) From this time on the tendency, already apparent in Pole, Varchi, Ossorio, and Jovius, to judge Machiavelli more by hear-say than by knowledge of his works became, naturally, very marked.

We have now to look for a moment at the French popular criticism of Machiavelli, which, as will be seen, was the main source of all the Elizabethan misunderstanding. In a pamphlet, falsely fathered upon Henri Estienne, [3]) Catherine de' Medici is accused of having brought Machiavelli's works to France. [4]) In 1576, Gentillet dedicated a refutation [5]) of the "Principe" to Alençon, and received nothing but ridicule from him in return. [6]) He ascribed to Machiavelli's [7]) writings, not only the massacre of St. Bar-

[1]) Cf. Burd 49.

[2]) So thorough was the suppression of his works that Lucchesini preaching against him at this time, could only read them by special Papal licence. Cf. Villari II, 414.

The second edition of the Cruscan Dictionary dared not name him, but citing him for the purity of his style, called him simply "un' secretario Fiorentino" cf. Farnew. I, 474.

[3]) Mark. Pattison: Essays I, 120.

[4]) "Catherine de' Medicis est Italienne et Florentine .... Les Florentins .... se soucient peu de leur conscience: veulent sembler religieux et non pas l'estre, faisons grand cas (comme aussi Machiavel, l'un de leurs premiers politiques, le conseille à son Prince) de ce qu'avoit jadis fort souvent en la bouche l'ambitieux Ixion,

Cherche d'avoir d'homme droit le renom,
Mais les effets et justes œuvres non.
Fay seulement cela dont tu verras
Que recevoir du profit tu pourras."

[5]) "Discours sur les Moyens de bien gouverner et maintenir en bonne paix un Royaume ou autre Principauté: Divisez en trois Parties; a savoir, du Conseil, de la Religion et Police que doit tenir un Prince: Contre Nicholas Machiavel, Florentin. A Treshaut et Tres-illustre Prince François Duc d'Alençon fils et frere de Roy. 1576."

[6]) Cf. La Popiliniere: Hist. des Hist. VII, 405.

[7]) "Dont l'on pourroit esbahir, que veut dire qu'on n'en parloit du

tholomew, [1]) but also the whole French policy, from Henry II
to Charles IX and Henry III, [2]) who were generally believed
to be well read in "the Queen-Mothers bible". [3])

Gentillet states the maxims of the „Principe" and
„Discorsi" very succinctly and very unfairly; for he says
nothing of why or how these books were constructed: his
refutations are rather long-winded, covering 639 pages.
As Mohl says, this work became the great arsenal, [4]) from

---

tout point en France du regne de François I, ny encores que fort peu
du regne du Roy Henry II, et que seulement depuis eux le nom de
Machiavel a commencé à estre cognu deça les monts, et ses escrits en
reputation. La response à cela n'est pas trop obscure à ceux qui savent
comment les afaires de France on esté gouvernez depuis le decez du feu
Roy Henry II, d'heureuse mémoire Car de son regne et auparavant
on s'estoit toujours 'gouverné à la Françoise, c'est à dire, en suyuant
les traces et enseignemens de nos ancestres François, mais depuis on
s'est gouverné à l'Italienne ou à la Florentine, c'est à dire, en suyuant
les enseignemens de Machiavel Florentin, comme nous verrons cy apres."
Gent. p. 8.

[1]) Villari II, 417.

[2]) Davila says Corbinelli used to read the Prince to Henry III.
Cf. Davila trans. Farneworth I, 402. Again: "Bourcher asserted that
Henry III carried him [Mach.] in his pocket: qui perpetuus ei in sacculo
atque manibus est: and Montaigne confirms the story when he says:
Et dict on, de ce temps, que Machiavel est encores ailleurs en crédit."
Acton, Intro. to Burd. XXIII.

[3]) "Some have related that Catharine de' Medici, Queen to Henry II
of France, made the "*Prince*" her particular study and put it into the
hands of her children" .... The author of the "*Tocsain contre les
Massacreurs*" p. 54 observes that Charles IX had been very ill edu-
cated .... the Queen caused her children to be taught such precepts
as were fitter for a Tyrant then a vertuous Prince, making them read
not only the foolish stories of Perceforest, but above all the treatise
[Il Principe] of that *Atheist Machiavel*, whose aim was to teach a
Prince rather how to make himself feared than beloved .... And indeed one may call that book the Queen-Motheris Bible."

Farnew. I, 489.

[4]) "Das Arsenal, aus welchem sie die Waffen gegen den Feind
holten, die selbst zu· schmieden sie zu träge waren." Mohl, Gesch. u.
Lit. d. Staatswis. III, 541.

which future would-be combatants drew their weapons. In this striking group of maxims, each expressed in two or three lines, Burd [1]) saw rightly the rise of so-called "Machiavellism". It is from this "Contre - Machiavel", published in 1576 (2 nd ed. 1579), translated into English in 1577, that the Elizabethan dramatists drew, far more than from Machiavelli himself; as did also the critics of the seventeenth and eighteenth centuries. For this reason, it is necessary to consider the main features of the work. Gentillet followed Jovius in proclaiming Machiavelli illiterate [2]) in the very subject he sought to expound, and in denouncing him as an atheist. [3]) His writings were made exclusively to inculcate tyranny: [4]) which no one ever knew better how to do. [5]) The zealous Frenchman declared the Florentine, "remply de toute meschanceté et ignorance"; that he was "banny et chassé de Florence"; that his life was most vicious, [6]) and that he had been the author "de mepris de Dieu, de perfidie, de Sodomie, tyrannie, cruauté, pilleries, usures estrangeres et autres vices destestables". He had

---

[1]) "These maxims were commonly accepted as an adequate summary, and it is impossible not to feel that they are, in a large degree, responsible for Machiavellism." Burd p. 54.

[2]) "Mais mon but est seulement de monstrer que Nicholas Machiavel Florentin .... n'a rien entendu, ou peu, en ceste science Politique .... que Machiavel a esté du tout ignorant en ceste science. .... Il n'avoit aussi point, ou peu de savoir aux Histoires." p. 3—4.

[3]) "Machiavell, qui s'est monstré par ses escrits un vray atheiste et contempteur de toute pieté." p. 14. "Machiavel, un vray atheiste et contempteur de Dieu." p. 141. This occurs again and again.

[4]) "De toutes ces choses Machiavel en traite en telle sorte qu'il est aisé à cognoistre que son but a esté d'instruire le Prince à estre un vray Tyran, et à luy enseigner l'art de Tyrannie." p. 251.

[5]) Bien veux-ie confesser qu'au gouvernement d'un estat de Tyrannie, Machiavel a esté mieux entendu que nul autre que i'aye leu, tant bien a-il sçeu tous les points et enseignements qui son propres pur l'establir, comme nous verrons cy apres en traitant ses maximes. p. 13.

[6]) "— il ne fut iamais homme au monde plus fouillé et contaminé de tous vices et meschancetez que luy." p. 5. cf. p. 623.

taught a prince "à se despouiller de toute pieté, conscience et Religion". By his doctrines also great wealth was to be acquired. [1]) All that was bad in his writings was his own: all the good had been stolen from Livy [2]) and Barthole. [3])

Since it will be necessary to keep always in mind the maxims taken from Machiavelli by Gentillet, they are here given exactly as in the first edition.

A) Maximes de la premiere partie, traitant du conseil que doit avoir un Prince.

1. Le bon conseil d'un Prince doit proceder de sa prudence mesme, autrement il ne peut estre bien conseille.
2. Le Prince, pour eviter flateurs, doit defendre a ceux de son conseil, qu'ils ne luy parlent ne donnent conseil, sinon des choses dont il leur entamera propos, et demandera avis.
3. Le Prince ne se doit fier aux estrangers.

B) Maximes de la seconde partie, traitant de la Religion que doit avoir un Prince.

1. Un prince, sur toutes choses, doit appeter d'estre estimé devot, bien qu'il ne le soit pas.

---

[1]) "Nous voyons a l'œil et touchons au doigt l'avarice des Italiens (Machiavellistes) qui nous mine et ruine et qui succe toute nostre substance, et ne nous laisse rien. Les uns ont le maniement des fermes, douanes, gabelles et domaines, a tel prix qu'ils veulent, et void on fondre les derniers entre leurs mains, sans qu'il apparoisse que rien, ou peu, soit converty au profit de la chose publique. Les autres attrapent les grands estats, offices et benefices, par le moyen desquels les deniers de France leur, es mains. Et ceux qui n'ont moyen de manier les afaires du public tiennent banques es bonnes villes, ou ils exercent usures immences et exorbitantes . . . . font souvent revenir leur deniers à raison de cinquante voire du cent pour cent." p. 15—16.

[2]) p. 6.

[3]) p. 251—254.

2. Le Prince doit soustenir ce qui est faux en la Religion, pourveu que cela tourne en faveur d'icelle.

3. La Religion des Payens leur tenoit le coeur haut et hardy à entreprendre grandes choses: mais la Religion des chrestiens les ramenant à humilité, leur affoiblit le coeur et les expose en proye.

4. Les grands Docteurs de la Religion Chrestienne, par grande obstination, ont tasché d'abolir la memoire des bonnes lettres et de tout antiquité.

5. Quand on delaissa la Religion Payenne le monde devint tout corrompu, et vint à ne croire plus ny Dieu ny Diable.

6. L'Eglise Romaine est cause de toutes les calamitez d'Italie.

7. Moyse n'eust jamais peu faire observer ses ordonnances, si main armee luy eust failly.

8. Moyse usurpa la Judee, comme les Goths usurperent partie de l'Empire Romain.

9. La Religion de Numa fut la principale cause de la felicité de Rome.

10. L'homme est heureux tant que fortune s'accorde à la complexion et humeur d'iceluy.

C) Maximes de la troisiesme partie, traitant de la police que doit avoir un Prince.

1. La guerre est juste qui est necessaire, et les rames raisonnables, quand on ne peut avoir esperance d'ailleurs.

2. Pour faire qu'un Prince retire du tout sa fantasie de faire paix en accord avec ses adversaires luy faut faire user de quelque tour outrageux contre iceux.

3. Un Prince en pays conquis doit establir Colonies, du moins en lieux plus forts, et en chasser les naturels habitans.

4. Le Prince en pays nouvellement conquis doit abbatre tous ceux qui souffrent grand' perte au changement, et du

tout exterminer le sang et la race de ceux qui auparavant dominoyent.

5. Pour se venger d'un pays ou d'une cité, sans coup ferir, la faut remplir de meschantes moeurs.

6. C'est folie de penser que nouveaux plaisirs facent oublier vieilles offences aux grands Seigneurs.

7. Le Prince se doit proposer à imiter Caesar Borgia fils du Pape Alexandre sixiesme.

8. Le Prince ne doit se soucier d'estre reputé cruel, pourveu qu'il se face obeir.

9 Mieux vaut à un Prince d'estre craint qu'aimé.

10. Le Prince ne se doit fier en l'amitié des hommes.

11. Le Prince qui veut faire mourir quelqu'un, doit cercher quelque couleur apparentre, et n'en sera point blasmé, pourveu qu'il laisse les biens aux enfans.

12. Le Prince doit ensuyure la nature du Lyon, et du Renard: non de l'un sans l'autre.

13. Cruauté qui tend à bonne fin n'est reprehensible.

14. Il faut qu'un Prince exerce cruauté tout en un coup, et face plaisir peu à peu.

15. Un Tyran vertueux pour maintenir sa tyrannie, doit entretenir partialitez entre ses sujets, et tuer les amateurs du bien public.

16. Un Prince peut aussi bien estre hay pour sa vertu, que pour son vice.

17. Le Prince doit tousiours nourrir quelque ennemy contre soy, afin que venant à l'opprimer, il en soit estimé plus grand et redoutable.

18. Le Prince ne doit craindre de se perjurer, tromper et dissimuler: car le trompeur trouve tousiours qui se laisse tromper.

19. Le Prince doit savoir cavaller les esprits des hommes pour les tromper.

20. Le Prince qui (comme par contrainte) usera de douceur et gracieuseté, avancera sa ruine.

21. Le Prince prudent ne doit observer la foy, quand

l'observation luy en est dommageable, et que les occasions qui la luy ont fait promettre sont passees.

22. La foy, clemence, liberalité sont vertus fort dommageables à un Prince; mais il est bon qu'il en ait le semblant tant seulement.

23. Le Prince doit avoir l'esprit dextrement habitué à estre cruel, inhumain et desloyal, pour se savoir monstrer tel, quand il est besoin.

24. Le Prince voulant rompre la paix promise et juree avec son voisin, doit mouvoir guerre et s'attacher contre l'amy d'iceluy.

25. Le Prince doit avoir le courage disposé à tourner selon les vents et variation de fortune, et se savoir servir du vice au besoin.

26. Chicheté est louable en un Prince, et la reputation de mechanique est un deshonneur sans malvueillance.

27. Le Prince qui voudroit fair estroitte profession d'homme de bien, ne pourroit estre de longue duree en ce monde, en la compagnie de tant d'autres qui ne valent rien.

28. Les hommes ne savent estre du tout bons ou du tout meschans, ny user de cruauté et violence parfaite.

29. Celuy qui a tousiours porté visage d'homme de bien, et veut devenir meschant pour parvenir à quelque degré, doit coulourer son changement de quelque raison apparente.

30. Le Prince en temps de paix entretenant partialité entre ses sujets, pourra par ce moyen les manier plus aisément à sa volonté.

31. Seditions et dissentions civiles sont utiles, et ne sont à blasmer.

32. Le moyen de tenir les sujets en paix et union, et les garder de se remuer, c'est de les tenir pauvres.

33. Le Prince qui craint ses sujets, doit bastir forteresses en son pays, pour les tenir en obeissance.

34. Le Prince doit deleguer à autruy les afaires dont

l'execution est sujette à inimitié et se reserver ceux qui despendent de sa grace.

35. Pour ministrer bonne justice, le Prince doit establir grand nombre de juges.

36. Les gentis-hommes qui tienent chasteaux et jurisdictions sont fort ennemis des Republiques.

37. La noblesse de France ruineroit l'estat du Royaume, si les Parlamens ne la punissoyent et tennoyent en crainte.

Such of these maxims as the dramatists used, will be compared with Machiavelli's own words later on: how viciously, and unjustly they were singled out, must be apparent to all students. An English translation, which will be discussed in its place, was immediately made. Having reached the source of Elizabethan Machiavellianism, it would be irrelevant, however interesting, to follow the general criticism of the Florentine farther.

I. Machiavelli in English Literature previous to the Drama.

Italy was over two hundred years ahead of any other modern nation in the renaissance; in the beginning of the 14th century she had produced Dante, Petrarca, and Boccaccio: less than two centuries later Machiavelli, Ariosto, and Tasso. These brilliant lights, accompanied by lesser luminaries, had all appeared before England,[1] Germany, France, and Spain, had emerged from medieval dusk.

England was the next country to awaken: naturally she turned towards Italy, to see what had been brought

---

[1] To be sure, Chaucer had lit up his country immediately after the first great Italian trio; but, when the glow of his genius died out, a very gloomy twilight set in.

forth, and, finding an abundant harvest of good fruit,
helped herself copiously. English poetry fashioned itself
after the Italian, just as the English gentleman adopted
the fashions of the Italian; but only until the novelty wore
off, and Englishmen perceived their own clothes were
stronger, fitted them better, allowed them to move more
comfortably, and even looked better on them than all the
foreign finery. In the middle of the 16th century there
was a perfect rush of Englishmen to Italy: they saw the
profligacy [2]) of the courts, and imbibed somewhat, at least,
of their contempt for true religion and of their corrupt
living.[3])

---

[1]) "The example of Italy was felt in all departments of study, in
every branch of intellectual activity. Three centuries ahead of us in
mental training, with Dante, Petrarch, Boccaccio, Ariosto and Tasso
already on their list of classics; boasting a multifarious literature of
novels, essays, comedies, pastorals, tragedies and lyrics; with their great
histories of Guicciardini and Machiavelli; with their political philosophy
and metaphysical speculations; the Italians — as it was inevitable —
swayed English taste, and moved the poets of England to imitation.
Surrey and Wyatt introduced the sonnet and blank verse from Italy
into England. Spenser wrote the "Faëry Queen" under the influence
of the Italian romantic epics. Raleigh could confer no higher praise on
this great poem than to say that Petrarch's ghost, no less than Homer's,
was moved thereby, to weeping for his laurels. Sidney copied the
Italians in his lyrics, and followed Sannazzaro in the Arcadia."
Symonds: Shak. Preds. 215.

[2]) "The [English] ladies spend the morning in devout prayer, not
resembling the gentlewoemen in *Italy*, who begin their morning at
midnoone, and make their evening at midnight, using sonnets for psalmes,
and pastime for prayers .... The Englysh Damoselles .... are as
cunning in ye scriptures as you are in Ariosto or Petrach .... They
in *England* pray when you play, sowe when you sleep, fast when you
feast, and weepe for their sins, when you laugh in your sensualitie."
Lyly: "Euphues" ed. Arber 442.

[3]) "— heare, what the Italian sayth of the English man, what
the master reporteth of the scholar: who uttereth plainlie what is
taught by him, and what learned by you, saying *Englese Italianato è
un diabolo incarnato*, that is to say, you remain men in shape and

(1568?)

However undesired this justly seemed to some, the tide continued to flow towards Italy:[1]) certainly, to the great benefit of English literature, if not of morals. Ascham himself had been in Italy, and his denunciation of the vicious life there, was that of many grave and sedate men. He was the first to mention Machiavelli,[2]) of whom he can have had but very little knowledge; for he accuses him of upholding catholicism!

„Yet though in Italie they [Englishmen] may freely be of no religion, as they are in Englande in verie deede to, neverthelesse returning home into England

---

facion, but become devils in life and condition. .... If some do not well understand what is an Englishe man Italianated, I will plainly tell him. He that by living, and traveling in *Italie*, bringeth home into England out of *Italie* the Religion, the learning, the policie, the experience, the manners of *Italie*. That is to say, for Religion, Papistrie or worse; for learning, lesse commonly than they carried out with them: for pollicie, a factious hart, a discoursing head, a minde to medle in all men's matters .... The Italian, that first invented the Italian proverbe against our Englishe men Italianated meant no more their vanitie in living, than their lewd opinion in Religion. For in calling them Deviles, he carieth them cleane away from God: and yet he carrieth them noe farder, than they willinglie go themselves, that is, where they may freely say their mindes, to the open contempte of God and all godliness, both in living and doctrine." Ascham: "Scholemaster" ed. Arber 78—81.

[1]) "It was thought that residence for some monthes in the chief Italian capitals was necessary to complete a young man's education; and though jealous moralists might shake their heads, averring that English lads exchanged in Italy their learning for lewd living, their religious principles for atheism, their patriotism for Machiavellian subtleties, their simplicities for affectations in dress and manners, yet the custom continued to prevail, until at last in the reign of the first Stuart, the English Court competed for the prize of immorality with the Courts of petty Southern princes." Symonds, Sh. Preds. 215.

[2]) P. Whitehorne had translated "The Arte of Warre" in 1560, but this relatively unimportant work remained apparently uncommented upon. Vide ante p. 2. Cf. Herbert III, 1311.

they must countenance the profession of the one or
the other, howsoever inwardlie, they laugh to scorne
both. And though, for their private matters they
can follow, fawne and flatter noble Personages,
contrarie to them in all respectes, yet commonlie
they allie themselves with the worst Papistes, to
whom they be wedded, and do well agree togither
in three proper opinions: In open contempt of Goddes
worde: in a secret securitie of sinne: and in a bloodie
desire to have all taken away, by sword and bur-
ning, that be not of their faction. They that do
read, with indifferent judgement, Pygius and Machiavel, two indifferent Patriarches of thies two Religions
do know full well what I say trewe." Ascham.
op. cit. 83.

This is merely an echo of the fierce diatribes, which
religious controversy [1]) had long ago called forth upon
Machiavelli.

Ascham wrote his "Scholemaster" after 1563 and before 1568; it was published in 1570. His assumption that
Machiavelli was known can apply only to scholars, for into
literature he had not yet found entrance.[2])

(1573)

Soon after Ascham's book, however, Machiavelli began
to interest English readers, as he had already done French.
The case of young Gabriel Harvey is typical of this movement: at twenty-three years of age in 1573, a student at
Cambridge, he had not read the Florentine's works, but was
eager to see them, and begged Remington to loan him
his copy.

"M. Remington, you remember I was in hand with
you not long agoe for your Machiavell, the greate

[1]) Vide ante p. 4.
[2]) Neither the popular pamphlets of the day, nor the works of
such "courtly makers" as Wyatt, Surrey, Grimoald, Berners, and their
immediate followers, indicate any knowledge whatever of Machiavelli.

Meyer, Machiavelli.

founder and master of pollicies. I praie you send me him now bi this schollar, and I wil dispatch him home againe, God willing, ere it be long, as politique I hope as I shal find him. For I purpose to peruse him only, not to misuse him: and superficially to surveie his forrests of pollicie, not guilefully to conveie awaie his interest in them. Although I feare me it had neede be a high point of pollicie, that should rob Master Machiavel of his pollicie, especially if the surveier be himself an straunger in the Italian territories. .... In good sadnes, M. Remington if ani dout greatly trubble me concerning the state of ani citti, or the condition of ani person (for I understand Machiavel is altogithers in his Italian stories) I am purposid to make bowld of you, and to crave your advise in the matter."[1])

Incontinently Harvey was perusing, and reperusing, Machiavelli and Aretine.[2])

"Owlde and yunge
For matter and tunge,

— — — —

Machiavell, Aretine, and whome you will,
That ar any waye renown'd for extraordinary skill;

— — — —

I reade and reade till I flinge them away,
And then goodnight studye, tomorrowe is hallidaye."

Op. cit. 135.

In this year also, appeared the second edition of Whitehorne's "Arte of Warre".[3])

(1574)

Sidney, too, had become acquainted with Machiavelli's works; probably at Oxford: in the next year, (1574), he

---

[1]) G. Harvey: Letterbook ed. Scott (Camb. Soc.) 1884. p. 174.

[2]) Aretine became as typical of sensuality, as Machiavelli of villainy, to the Elizabethans. The number of references to him is simply legion.

[3]) Cf. Herbert II, 1064.

facetiously applies one of the remarks in the „Principe" to his Languet, for censuring the English too severely.

"Nunquam adduci poteram, ut crederem Machiavellum bene d/e nimiâ clementiâ fugiendâ sensisse, donec usu idem mihi venerit, quod ille multis rationibus probare conatus est.[1])

Languet, in answer, jocosely calls Machiavelli Sidney's friend.[2])

"I admire the candour with which you warn me to beware of you, for that is the meaning of your fierce threats. But there you do not follow the advice of your friend Machiavelli, unless perhaps it is fear that has extorted those big and sounding words, and you thought that so I might be deterred from my intentions."[3])

The quotations, hitherto made from English authors (Ascham's [4]) case excepted), show not the slightest tendency to misinterpret or denounce Machiavelli: this is very significant. In 1576 appeared Gentillet's „Anti-Machiavel", which, as has been seen, heaped all possible ignominy upon the Florentine.

(1577)

In the following year (1577), an English translation was made of Gentillet's book by Simon Patericke,[5]) and

---

[1]) Sidney to Languet. Padua 29th April 1574. Letters ed. Pears, 215.

[2]) It is interesting to note Symonds "Sir Ph. Sid." (198). „He was equally removed from servility to his sovereign, and from the underhand subtleties of a would-be Machiavelli."

[3]) Ibid. 71 (translated by Pears from Latin).

[4]) It must be remembered Ascham was influenced more by the old religious controversy than by knowledge of Machiavelli.

[5]) He was an Englishman of Caister, Lincolnshire, notwithstanding he says in the "Epis. Ded." "I never saw England." Account of him in Cooper: Athen. Catab. II, 496, where is noted — "It is remarkable that the translator speaks of himself as never having visited England." Vide also: Dic. Nat. Biog. ad loco.

dedicated to Francis Hastings and Edward Bacon: the first
edition appeared in 1602; the second in 1608. Both are
exactly alike; containing all of Gentillet, except the dedication to Alençon and the verses following. It is best to
let the translator himself explain his object in presenting
Gentillet to English readers.

"For then" [before the Queen-Mother brought Machiavelli into France] „Satan being a disguised person
amongst the French, in the likenesse of a merrie
jester, [Rabelais] acted a comoedie, but shortly
ensued a wofull Tragoedie. When our countrymen's
minds were sick, and corrupted with these pestilent
diseases, and that discipline waxed stale; then came
forth the books of *Machiavel*, a most pernitious
writer, which beganne not in secret and stealing
manner (as did those former vices) but by open
meanes, and as it were a continual assault, utterly
destroyed not this or that vertue, but even all
vertues at once: Insomuch as it took faith from
Princes; authoritie and majesty from laws: libertie
from the people; and peace and concord from all
persons, which are the only remedies for present
malladies. For what shall I speake of Religion
whereof the Machiavellians had none, as alreadie
plainly appeareth, yet they greatly laboured also to
deprive us of the same.

. . . . Moreover Sathan useth strangers of France,
as his fittest instruments, to infect us still with
this deadly poison sent out of Italy, who have so
highly promoted their Machiavellian bookes, that he
is of no reputation in the court of France, which hath not
Machiavel's writings at his finger's ends, and · that
both in the Italian and French tongues, and can
apply his precepts to all purposes, as the Oracles of
Apollo. Truly, it is a wonderful thing to consider
how faste that evill weede hath growne within these

fewe yeares, seeing there is almost none that striveth
to excell in vertue or knowledge: as though the
only way to obtain honour and riches were by this
deceiver's direction. . . . . She, the most renowned
Queen [Elizabeth] hath hitherto preserved the state
of her realme, not only safe but flourishing, not by
Machiavellian artes, as Guile, Perfidie and other
Villainies practising, but by true vertues, as Cle-
mencie, Justice, Faith . . . . But O how happy are
yee, both because you have so gratious a Queene,
and also for that the infectious Machiavellian doctrine,
hath not breathed nor penetrated the intrailes of
most happy England. But that it might not so do,
I have done my endeavor, to provide an antidote
and present remedie, to expell the force of so deadly
poyson, if at any time it chance to infect you. . . . .
Kalends Augusti Anno 1577.[1])

Thus we see, Patericke believed Machiavelli (whom
he evidently knew only from Gentillet), sent from Sathan
to France, had made a hell of it, where his doctrines were
in everyone's mouth. But of paramount importance is
that he expressly states, Machiavelli was not known in
England up to 1577, and that he speaks of "riches obtained
by this deceiver's direction".

These fierce denunciations of Gentillet and Patericke
had an immediate effect upon English readers.

(1578)

In 1578 appeared a work [2]) by Harvey, one poem of
which, supported by several others, may be viewed as the
direct outgrowth of the Gentillet-Patericke diatribes.

The part in question runs as follows:

---

[1]) "The Epistle Dedicatorie."

[2]) "XAIᐧPE: Gabrielis Harveij Gratulationum Valdinensium Libri
quattuor. London 1578." Lib. I to Elizabeth; II to Leicester; III to
Burleigh; IV to Hatton. A propos of Burleigh, readers of Disraeli will
remember he nick-named the great minister "Machiavel" in his "Ame-
nities of Literature".

Epigramma in effigiem Machiavelli.

Machiavellus ipse loquitur.

Quaeris, ego qui sim? Rex Regum: totius orbis [1]
    Imperium digito nititur omne meo.
Nemo regat, qui non Machavellica dogmata callet:
    Nec sapuisse putes qui minus ista sapit.
Caetera sunt umbrae, fumi, ludibria, risus, [5]
    Regna ego sola loquor, sceptra ego sola loquor,
Pacem optent pueri, vetulaeque, senesque, miselli,
    Castra ego sola loquor, bella ego sola loquor.
Plebis amor nihil est; nihilo minus, Indiga Virtus:
    Verba ego linquo alijs; facta ego mira patro. [10]
Ecce oculos: Furor ijs habitat: manus altera saxum;
    Altra ensem torquet: toxica in ore latent.
Spiritus hinc, atque hinc perfusus mille venenis:
    Ferrea frons, Orci pectora digna Deo.
Emblema est, semperque fuit: *Iuuat ire per altum:* [15]
    Aut nihil, aut Caesar; noster Alumnus erat.
Nil mediôcre placet: sublimia sola voluto:
    Lac pueris cibus est: sanguine vescor ego.
Mille neces obeat vulgus, modò sceptra capessam;
    Non flocci cruor est, non laniena mihi. [20]
Dispereant abiectae animae: trudantur ad Orcum:
    Solus ego sapio, vivo, triumpho mihi.
Caetera quis nescit? *Fraus* est mea maxima Virtus:
    Proxima, *Vis*: alios non ego nosco Deos.
Ingenij monumenta a mei Regalia volue: [25]
    Nec post hac quaeres: Quis Machavellus erat![1])

This is simply Gentillet epitomised; here we have the four principal crimes, ascribed to Machiavelli later on in the drama: poison, murder, fraud and violence. Especially is poison (line 13) to be noted; for the Florentine himself nowhere expressly recommends its use. It became, however, the prime factor in Elizabethan Machiavellianism. Lines 18 and 20 read as if they had been written after the appearance of Barabas, Aaron, Eleazar, and Lorenzo, instead of many years before them. But of tantamount importance is the heading:

                   "*Machiavellus ipse loquitur.*"

_____

[1]) Lib. II. p. 8.

Marlowe certainly had this before him, when he first brought Machiavelli in person upon the stage to speak the prologue to the "Jew of Malta". The line: —

"*Aut nihil, aut Caesar:* noster Alumnus erat."

no doubt suggested: —

"What right had Caesar to the empery?" [1]

In another epigram, [2] Mercury complains of Machiavelli; and Jupiter proclaims him a god co-potent, and the son of Maia. [3] Mercury incidentally remarks, that Machiavelli's teachings are not new: — "prisca novata iuuant"; [4] Gentillet had already asserted this. [5] In another place, the Florentine is called: "Deus rigidi Tyranni": [6] Gentillet laid especial stress upon this point. [5]

Again in "Medicaeorum Hymnus", after the gods are called upon to worship Machiavelli: —

"Juppiter annuerat: plausumque dedêre minores
    Dijque, Deaeque: novo sacrificantque Deo.
Sacrificaturos Deus ipse affatur amicos:
    O Dij, quanta Dea est *Fraus* comitata Dolis?
Non miranda Dea est, cui coeli Essentia quinta,
    Quattuor atque parent terrae elementa Deae?
Hinc ego divinis cumulatus honoribus, inter
    Reges, atque Deos, Rex color, atque Deus.
Hinc manibus supera, ima fero; septemque Planaetas,
    Bis septem Reges, Pontificesque meis.

---

[1] "Jew of Malta" Marlowe ed. Dyce 145.
[2] G. Harveij Mercurius Florentinus, vel Machiavelli ἀποθέωσις.
[3]   "— Hic, ait [Mercurius] alter ego est.
    Juppiter arrisit; Maia indignata parumper
        Mox ait: ergo etiam filius iste meus.
    Assensêre Dei, atque Deae: Machavellus atque uno
        Cunctorum assensu; Mercurius Deus est."
                                        Lib. II p. 10.
[4] Lib. II p. 9.
[5] Vide ante p. 7.
[6] Lib. II p. 10.

Mortales, reliquorum hominum comburite scripta;
  Solus ego Reges, Regnaque vestra rego.
Dixit: at excepit Pallas Britannica regna:
  Contiquitque Deus, contiquitque Dea."

The next to the last line is exactly what Patericke
said in his translation of Gentillet;[1]) Harvey has the
thought again in an epigram to Hartwell.[2]) Other in-
stances of contiguity might be given; but surely, those
cited are enough to show, Harvey must have had Gentillet
before him, and that probably in the MS. translation of
Patericke.

One line of the last passage is worthy of note:

"Vulpe, Leone, Apro, trux Machavelle, tuo."

Here is the Fox and Lion theory so often used in the
drama; and linked to it is "Apro", typical to Elizabethans
of concupiscence,[3]) which Machiavelli nowhere advocates,
but especially warns against.[4]) As will be seen, Lodge
accepted Harvey's idea, though he must have known
better.

(1579)

The rapidity, with which Machiavelli came into favor

---

[1]) Vide ante p. 16.

[2]) "Perplacuit paucis tecum, Machavelle, iocari:
  O Florentinus floreat ore lepos.
Rideo ego; plorare tibi licet, atque licebit,
  Quod procul est Princeps, ô Machavelle, tuus.
Nostra aliam ad formam Princeps fabricata, sereno,
  Non Tragico populos aspicit ore, suos.
Haud ita gestirent cives, veniente Tyranno,
  Vulpe, Leone, Apro, trux Machavelle, tuo.
Terribilis tua pompa nimis, non Barbara nobis,
  Turcica non rabies, non laniena placet."
                                        lib. I p. 7.

[3]) Post.)   Perchance he spoke not; but,
  Like a full-acorn'd boar, a German one,
  Cry'd, oh! and mounted: Cymbeline II, 5.

[4]) Vide "Principe" XVII and XIX.

at Cambridge, and the extent to which he was read, is remarkable: in 1579, Harvey claimed his works had supplanted all others, spoke of "an odd crewe or tooe as cuninge" in the same, and made the first hint at the harm private persons were acquiring from them.

"And I warrant you sum good fellowes amongst us begin nowe to be prettely well acquayntid with a certayne parlous booke callid, as I remember me, Il Principe di Niccolo Machiavelli, and I can peradventure name you an odd crewe or tooe that ar as cuninge in his Discorsi sopra la prima Deca 'di Livio, in his Historia Fiorentina, and in his Dialogues della Arte della Guerra tooe, and in certayne gallant Turkishe Discourses tooe, as University men were wont to be in their parva Logicolia and Magna Moralia and Physicalia of both sortes: *verbum intelligenti sat:*" Letter-book ed. Scott p. 79.

Now Greene was a student at Cambridge in this year, and Marlowe in the next: although the words quoted are, no doubt, exaggerated, and cannot be positively proved to apply to Greene and his associates, yet later testimony points clearly that way; for Harvey accuses both the dramatists of having used Machiavellian principles in their profligate lives, and Greene confesses it true.

In the same year Harvey informed Spencer: — "Machiavel a great man"[1] at Cambridge, and Italian studies flourishing.

(1580)

In 1580, he mentioned Machiavelli as a writer of co-

---

[1] „I beseech you all this while, what news at *Cambridge*. *Tully* and *Demosthenes* nothing so much studied as they were wont: . . . . *Machiavel* a great man: Castilio, of no small repute: *Petrarck* and *Boccaccio* in every man's mouth: Galateo and Guazzo never so happy: overmany acquainted with *Unico Aretino*." Harvey to Spencer 1579. Church: *"Spencer"* 25.

medies, [1]) praised him highly, but spoiled it all by ranking
Bibiena alongside. In this year, also, Thomas Lodge introduced Machiavelli into the popular controversial literature
of the day, with his immediately suppressed pamphlet: "A
Reply to Stephen Gosson's Schoole of Abuse"

> "— *latet anguis in herba*, under your fare show of
> conscience take heede you cloake not your abuse,
> it were pittie the learned should be overseene in
> your simplenesse, I feare me you will be politick
> wyth *Machavel* not zealous as a prophet." Lodge
> ed. Gosse III, 22.

To argue on the orthography of a word in Elizabethan
literature is very fallible, especially in this case; for Machiavelli's name was spelt in over an hundred different ways:
but it is worthy of note that Lodge here, and here alone,
adopts Harvey's spelling in the epigrams. He was then a
student at Oxford: his work shows no acquaintance at all
with Machiavelli's writings: he probably knew of him from
Harvey or Gentillet, assumed the same knowledge in his
public, cited him, and thus started a "craze", which really
became one in the fullest sense of the word, *viz.* to make
a scare-crow scape-grace of the Florentine's name on every
conceivable occasion. Lodge referred to Machiavelli as an
advocate of dissembling: this is simply Maxim 18. [2])

(1581)

In the next year, Barnaby Riche adapted Machiavelli's
novelette "Belphegor" in his "Farewell to the Militarie Pro-

---

[1]) "I am void of all judgement, if your *Nine Comedies* .... come
not nearer Ariosto's comedies .... than that *Elvish Queen* doth to
his *Orlondo Furioso* .... Besides that you know, it hath been the
usual practice of the most exquisite and odd wits .... rather to show,
and advance themselves that way than any other: as, namely those
three notorious discoursing heads, Bibiena, Machiavel, and Aretino
did .... being indeed reputed in all points matchable .... either with
Aristophanes and Menander in Greek, or with Plautus and Terence in
Latin." Harvey to Spencer.

[2]) Cf. Gentillet ante 9.

fession"; [1] and Thomas Howell reiterated the citation of
Lodge:

> "Provyde in youth, thy aged yeares to keepe,
> And let fayre speeche go lulle the fonde a sleepe,
> Sir *Machiavell* such cunning nowe hath tought.
> That wordes seeme sweete when bitter is the thought.
>
> — — — —
>
> Take heede therefore, retyre in time from those,
> To serve their turnes, that teach their tongues to glose,
> Whose golden shews, although do promise much,
> In proofe fall out but copper in the touch."
>
> Ed. Grosart. "Delightful Disc." 221.

(1583)

Hitherto, Machiavelli has been cited only as an author:
in 1583 Robert Greene was the first to make in popular
literature an abstract noun of the Florentine's name. Green
had been long in Italy, and was well read in the Italian
poets, in Guicciardini and Machiavelli, but in his use
of the latter he seems to have sacrificed his own knowledge to that panderism to public taste and feeling, which
was so characteristic of the gifted writer. On the very
first page of "Mamillia", praising the superior sturdiness of
Padua in not yielding to her enemies as Venice, Florence,
Sienna and other cities had done, Greene cited Machiavelli
as his authority: — "as Machiavell in his Florentine
history maketh report" (ed. Grosart II, 13). Further along
in the second part occurs this sentence: —

> "So Pharicles although he was whollie wedded unto
> vanitie, and had professed himselfe a mortall foe to

---

[1] As Warton said, "Even Machiavelli, who united the liveliest
wit with the profoundest reflection .... condescended to adorn this
fashionable species of writing with his "Novella di Belfegor"."
Hist. Eng. Poet. IV. 339.

Riche's tale of Mildred and the devil Balthazar is an ingenious
adaptation of "Belphegor" in a satire on the craze for new fashions.
As Collier says: "it may be considered the most original part of the
volume.". Riche ed. Collier Shak. Soc. 33. XVI.

vertue, being in the state of his life such a mutable
Machiavilian, as he neither regarded friend nor faith
oath nor promise, if his wavering wit perswaded him
to the contrary." [1]) ibid. 205.

It is perfectly plain, Greene had forgotten his own
study of Machiavelli, and was catering to popular sentiment. The thought is simply Maxim 18, introduced by
Lodge and Howell, coupled with Maxim 25: [2]) for Greene
lays stress upon the fact that his dissembler was very
mutable. [3])

(1584)

In the next year (1584), came out anonymously [4])
"Leycester's Commonwealth"; Sidney, who immediately wrote
a refutation of it, said the author "plays the statist, wringing
very unluckily some of Machiavel's axioms to serve his
purpose". [5]) But these axioms were not unluckily wrung:
Parsons cited Machiavelli thrice, and went each time to
the "Principe", of which he gave almost the very words.
The first reference is as follows: —

> "I doubt not, but my Lord of Leycester will take
> good heed, in joyning by reconciliation with *Huntington*,
> after so long a breach: and will not be so improvi-
> dent, as to make him his soveraigne, who now is
> but his dependent. Hee remembreth too well the

---

[1]) On which Grosart remarks: "*Machavilian* = after Machiavelli,
who for long was (preposterously) held to be the incarnation of all
deceitfulness. Professor Villari's recent erudite and judicious Life has
lifted off the centuries-old obloquy." It escaped Grosart that Greene
here puns on the name; it was pronounced, Match a villain, as will be
shown later on.

[2]) Gentillet ante 9.

[3]) Cf. Crowne: "Juliana" III (Dram. of Rest. I, 57).
Cassonofsky (when Lubomirsky shifts his policy)
> "So, there's Machiavel policy in the abstract; the wind of to'ther
> party blows a little dust in's teeth, and he wheels about."

[4]) In 1641 attributed to Father Parsons.

[5]) Misc. Works ed. Gray 311.

successe of the lord *Stanley* who helped King Henry
the seventh to the Crowne; of the Duke of *Buckingham*, who did the same for *Richard* the third; . . . .
All which Noble men upon occasions that after fell
out; were rewarded with death, by the selfe same
Princes, whom they had preferred. And that not
without reason as Siegnior *Machavel* my Lords Coun-
cellour affirmeth. For that such Princes, after ward
can never give sufficient satisfaction to such friends,
for so great a benefit received. And consequently
least upon discontentment, they may chance doe as
much for others against them, as they have done for
them against others: the surest way is, to recompence
them with such reward, as they shall never after
bee able to complain of." [1])

In the second notice, he said, Leicester was able, —
"to plunge his friend [Norfolk] over the eares in
suspition and disgrace, in such sort, as he should
never be able to draw himselfe out of the ditch
againe, as indeed he was not, but died in the same.
And herein you see also the same subtle and
Machiavilian sleight, which I mentioned before, of
driving men to attempt somewhat, whereby they
may incure danger, or remaine in perpetuall suspition
or disgrace. And this practice hee hath long used:
and doth daily, against such as he hath will to
destroy." [2])

The last citation was even more direct:
"For it is a setled rule of Machivel, which the
Dudlies doe observe: *That, where you have once done
a great injury, there you must never forgive.*" [3])

---

[1]) Leys. Com. (1641) 92. Cf. Prin. III: Disc. II, 33 (265): Ist.
Fior. IV (253).

[2]) Ibid. 149. Cf. Prin. VII. Gent. III, 11.

[3]) Ibid. 177. Cf. Prin. VII; Disc. III, 4 (312): Ist. Fior. IV (217).
Gent. III, 6.

Leicester was also accused of having poisoned many people, as well as of all villainy. This book ¹) of Parsons was wide read: we shall find these three maxims, and the poison principle (already in Gentillet), cropping out in the drama. ²)

II. Machiavelli in the Drama.

(1588)

The next author to mention Machiavelli, and the first to introduce him onto the stage, was Marlowe in 1588 in his "Jew of Malta". But now that the drama has been

---

¹) No better example could be given of the difference between this legitimate use of Machiavelli and the vicious popular mis-use than, anticipating about 40 years, by quoting the following stanza from a poem, "Leicesters Ghost", appended to an edition of "Leycester's Commonwealth" in 1641, but written about the end of the reign of James I, who is mentioned as alive: —

1) "Are there not some among you Parasites,
2) Time-servers and observers of no measure,
3) Prince-pleasers, people-pleasers, hypochrites.
4) Damn'd Machevillians given to lust and pleasure,
5) Church robbers, beggars of the Princes treasure,
6) Truce breakers, Pirats, Atheists, Sychophants,
7) Can equity dwell here, where conscience wants."

[In one of the two Brit. Mus. copies line 3 is made 5 and garbled thus: —

"Prince smothers, people pleasure, Hippochrites."]

It is almost needless to say, that in all Machiavelli's writings there are no directions for "parasites, time-servers, those given to lust and pleasure, church-robbers etc. etc."

²) Another episode, which Scott immortalised, also got onto the stage. In "The Yorkshire Tragedy" V (Anc. Brit. Dram. 433) the Husband exclaims when throwing the maid down stairs, —

"The surest way to charm a woman's tongue,
Is — break her neck: a politician did it"

Here "politician" is used in the same sense as Machiavilian.

reached the question naturally arises, was there any Machiavellianism in English dramatic literature before this introduction of the Florentine himself by Marlowe. Simpson, in his excellent essay on "The Political Use of the Stage in Shakspere's Time", makes the following remark: —

> "Tancred and Gismunda", partly by Hatton, afterwards Lord Chancellor, was acted before Queen Elizabeth in 1568. It is remarkable for its protests against tyranny, and for the hateful display of a tyrant in Tancred, with his simple maxims, such as
>
> > "This is the soundest safety for a king,
> > To cut off all that vex or hinder him"
>
> Tancred introduces us to what was the great political bugbear of the 16 th century — The Machiavellian. Marlowe confesses in his prologue that he means his *Jew of Malta* to exhibit that ideal: and from this we may see that Selimus in the *Tragical reign of Selimus sometime emperor of the Turks*, Aaron in *Titus Andronicus*, and the other characters in other plays, including perhaps Iago in *Othello* are intended for exhibitions of the hated and dreaded ideal. Most of them have this in common, that they confide their atrocious intentions and principles to the audience with the flattest simplicity and most elaborate self-analysis. Middleton's play *The Old Law* belongs to this type of political dramas."
>
> New Sh. Soc. II, 371.

To see in Tancred a Machiavellian is anticipating: between him and the true Machiavellians (Barabas, Aaron Eleazar, Richard III, Alphonsus etc.) there is a vast difference. The former is a firmly established tyrant, the latter are unscrupulous villains, seeking to establish themselves as tyrants, but invariably failing.

The character of a tyrant is one of the oldest in all dramatic literature, ancient and modern. Sidney speaks of how the classical drama „maketh kings fear to be tyrants, and tyrants to manifest their tyrannical humours".[1] "Tancred and Gismunda" is an out and out imitation of Seneca; the maxim quoted is the only one in the play which sounds Machiavellian, and may be found in Plutarch, Tacitus, Seneca,[2] and Aristotle: the principle is time-honored, forming the very *Leitmotiv* of "Cambyses".

The nearest approach to a Machiavellian before Barabas, was Lorenzo in the "Spanish Tragedy"; an arch-villain,[3] who uses Serberine in the murder of Horatio, bribes Pedringano to shoot Serberine, and has the assassin hung before he can expose all.

Lorenzo) "Thus must we work, that will avoid distrust,
Thus must we practice to prevent mishap:
And thus one ill another must expulse.

— — — —

And better 'tis that base companions die,
Than by their life to hazard our good haps;
Nor shall they live, for me to fear their faith;
I'll trust myself, myself shall be my friend;
For die they shall, slaves are ordain'd to no other end."[4]

Lorenzo is certainly the fore-runner, though at a great distance, of Barabas and Richard III. His lines: —

"Where words prevail not, violence prevails;
But gold doth more than either of them both." ibid. II.

---

[1] R. Fischer: "Zur Kunstentwickelung der Eng. Trag." p. 50.
[2] Cf. Duchess of Newcastle: "The Presence" I, 1 (2).
"Why, *Seneca* doth express Moral Virtues, and Machiavellian Policy, better and more properly then Dramatick Poetry."
[3] "Von Charakterentwickelung ist wenig zu merken; meist treten uns die Charaktere gleich fertig entgegen, und werden nur immer von einer Seite gezeigt: Lorenzo z. B. giebt sich von seinem ersten Auftreten an als Schurke aus Princip; stets erscheint er als Todfeind der Liebhaber seiner Schwester, und warum er Bellimperias Liebesglück zerstört, fragt sich der Zuschauer vergebens."
Markscheffel. T. Kyd. 13.
[4] Span. Trag. III (Dods. 74). A method, advocated in Prin. VII, employed by all Elizabethan Machiavellians.

are the very key-note of the Jew of Malta's character;
and the line just quoted: —

"I'll trust myself, myself shall be my friend."

is identical in thought with Richard's III famous: —

"I am myself alone."

and Barabas phrase corrupted from Terence: —

"*Ego mihimet sum semper proximus.*"

which is the very pith and gist of all Machiavelli's teachings.[1]
And again; Lorenzo knows: —

"Our greatest ills we least mistrust, my lord,
And inexpected harms do hurt us most."[2]

upon which Machiavelli lays especial stress.

Thus, the safe conclusion is that Kyd used the "Principe"
in portraying Lorenzo, but did not brand him a "Machiavel"
since, as we have seen, the mere name had as yet (1587?)
no terror for a popular audience.

The most colossal figures to be met with in the
Elizabethan drama, are Marlowe's Tamburlaine, Faustus,
and Barabas: into these Titans he breathed the very soul
of his existence, — a wild craving for infinite power. He
was the "notable exception" among the Elizabethan
dramatists; for he had studied Machiavelli with a
vengeance:[3] and it may be stated as an absolute certainty,

---

[1] Cf. Lee: "Caesar Borgia" III (ed. 1734 II, 50).
Machiavel) "I love myself: and for myself, I love
    Borgia my Prince: Who does not love himself?
    Self-Love's the universal Beam of Nature,
    The Axle-tree that darts thro' all its Frame."
Cf. also Steele in „Tatler" 186.
[2] III 83. .Cf. Prin. III: Disc. I, 2 (101); Ist. Fior. VII (151).
[3] Goethe and Marlowe had much of "those brave translunary
things" in common; besides their marvellously sympathetic attraction

Meyer, Machiavelli.

that had the "Principe" never been written, his three great
heroes would not have been drawn with such gigantic
strokes. Brandl has so consummately stated the general
influence of Machiavelli upon Marlowe, that, to add one
word, would be impudence.

„Ueber aufstrebende Herrschernaturen hatte niemand
so fein und eingehend gehandelt wie Macchiavelli, der
politische Klassiker des Cinquecento, dessen Lehren an den
Höfen fleifsig ins Praktische übersetzt wurden. Marlow
kannte ihn und liefs ihn im "Jew of Malta" als prolocutor
auftreten. Auch die Warnung des sterbenden Greene an
Marlow setzt ihn als bekannt voraus: "Is it pestilent
Machivilian policy that thou hast studied?" (Marlow ed.
Dyce XXVII.) Doppelt beachtenswert sind daher die
mannigfachen Übereinstimmungen zunächst zwischen Mac-
chiavellis "Principe" und Marlows "Tamerlan".

Um mit Tamerlans Gegnern zu beginnen: Mycetes,
der schwache Perserkönig, nimmt sich wie eine Illustration
des angestammten Fürsten aus, der nach Macchiavelli
(Principe, Kap. 2) die Krone nur verlieren kann, wenn un-
gewöhnliche äufsere Gewalt herantritt und er selbst durch
aufserordentliche Lasten sich verhafst macht. Von aufsen

---

to the Faust legend, each was powerfully drawn to Machiavelli in his
youth. In 1774 the young Goethe writes to Lavater: —

"So ist das Wort der Menschen mir Wort Gottes .... und mit
inniger Seele falle ich dem Bruder um den Hals, Moses,
Prophet, Evangelist, Apostel, Spinoza oder Machiavell." Vide
J. Schmidt: "Goethe's Stellung zum Christenthum" Jahrb. II, 57.

In his "Tagebuch" for 30 July 1807 occurs this: —

"Alles Spinozistische in der poetischen Production wird in der
kritischen Reflexion Macchiavellismus" Weim. Ausg. III, 250.

And in Egmont the secretary to the "Regentin Margarete" is
called Machiavel; although this was an historical personage, (which
Ward I, 186 did not know), Goethe certainly chose this one among the
insignificant characters for the significance of the name.

bedrängen ihn die Türken und Tartaren, im Innern weckt ihm sein tyrannisches Verfügen über das Leben eines Vasallen Mifstrauen (A. I Sc. 1).

Thronraub, soviel Greuel damit auch verbunden sein mögen, ist nach Macchiavelli nichts unnatürliches und pflegt sogar Bewunderung zu ernten, wenn der Mann sich nur zu halten vermag. Tadelnswert aber ist, wer darnach gestürzt wird, und das wird dem passieren, der nicht mit eigener Kraft ausreicht oder gar einen sehr mächtigen Fremden hereinruft. Er mufs schöne Worte machen, hat im Notfall nicht die rechte Gewalt über seine Anhänger und hängt vom Glücke ab. (Principe Cap. 3. 6.) Dieser Klasse gehört Cosroe an. Am Hofe des Mycetes ist er als Redner bekannt; durch schöne Versprechungen erreicht er auch, dafs ihm seine Mitvasallen die Krone des Mycetes übertragen: "my lord" sagt er zu einem derselben. Ohne ausreichende Stütze in sich selbst vertraut er sich den "approved Fortunes" Tamerlans an (A. II Sc. 3) und wähnt ihn zu seinem bescheidenen Bundesgenossen machen zu können, worauf ihn dieser Gigant natürlich abschüttelt, besiegt und sterben läfst (A. II Sc. 6).

Erfolg hat nach Macchiavelli nur, wer die Eigenschaft und Geistesgröfse besitzt, seine Anhänger dauernd zu beherrschen; der empfängt vom Glücke blofs die Gelegenheit. Diesem Ideal eines zur höchsten Macht emporstrebenden Mannes entspricht Tamerlan Zug für Zug. "I am a lord", erklärt er, der geborene Schäfer, in richtiger Selbsterkenntnis, "for so my deeds shall prove." Er verschmäht es, "to play the orator". Seine Anhänger sind ihm „friends and followers". "His fortunes majster" nennt ihn sogar der Gegner (A. II Sc. 1). Dafs er grofs, wenn auch barbarisch denkt, zeigt er in der Liebeswerbung um die gefangene Zenocrate, welche nur in der Werbung Richards III. um die des Gatten beraubte Anna ihres Gleichen hat (A. I Sc. 2). Was nur Macchiavelli einem Tyrannen zur Befestigung seiner Macht empfiehlt, also: Beseitigung der Neider, Strenge gemischt mit Grofsmut und Klugheit, stete Schlagfertigkeit und fortgesetzte Feldzüge, besonders auch Abhärtung der Söhne (Prin. Cap. 40),[1]) wird von Tamerlan in den übrigen Akten ausgeführt, so dafs er im Bette stirbt und seinen Söhnen ein gesichertes Reich hinterläfst; höchster Triumph eines Macchiavellischen Emporkömmlings! Lerne, ruft Tamerlan, am Schlusse seinem Ältesten zu, einen so gefährlichen Thron bewahren; bist du nicht nicht voll Feuergedanken, werden dich diese rebellischen Gäule bei der nächsten Gelegenheit abwerfen; "the nature of thy chariot will not bear a guide of baser temper than myself". Ein innerer Konflikt ist nicht versucht; aber man sieht, wie Macchiavelli in der Zeichnung des bisher hohlen und starren Tyrannentypus einen psychologischen Fortschritt anregt, stufenweise Entwickelung anbahnt und allgemeine Rhetorik à la Seneca durch reale Züge und Gegensatzfiguren durchbricht.

Barabas gehört einer Klasse von Emporkömmlingen an, welche Macchiavelli minder ausführlich beschrieben hat, und doch läfst ihn Macchiavelli auf die Bühne geleiten, als einen Träger des gleichen Geistes, desselben gewissenlosen Strebens nach Macht. Der Jude gehört zu der Gattung der Bestechungstyrannen: sein Können liegt im Golde. Zu einer eigentlichen Krone gelangen zu wollen, hat Macchiavelli solchen Leuten misraten, weil gekaufte Anhänger wandelbar und unzuverlässig sind (Prin. Cap. 7). Das weifs Barabas: "nothing violent, oft have I heard tell, can be permanent". Er hat nicht die von Macchiavelli geforderte Eigenkraft, verzichtet daher auf ein Gewaltunternehmen. Wenn ihn die Natur schliefslich doch dazu treibt, mit verzweifelter Schlauheit und Energie die Herrschaft über Malta an sich zu reifsen, stürzt ihn gerade der Verrat eines gekauften Helfers, so wie es Macchiavelli geweissagt hatte.

---

[1]) There is some discrepancy here; the "Principe" contains but 26 chapters, and nowhere in it is "Abhärtung der Söhne" advocated!

Noch vager wird die Nachwirkung des Macchiavelli im „Faust": Auch Faust kauft die höchste Macht, um schliefs- lich durch die natürliche Unzuverlässigkeit solcher Macht- stützen alles zu verlieren. — Für die Figur des Guise in der „Bluthochzeit" ist hier wenigstens anzuführen, dafs Macchiavelli in seiner Vorrede zum "Jew of Malta". sagt, er fühle sich in ihm fortleben. Auch bot für die Umgestal- tung des Guise und Mortimer die englische und schottische Geschichte der letzten Jahrzehnte nicht zu unterschätzende Modelle in Bothwell und Leicester."[1])

Thus, then, was the general influence upon Marlowe himself:[2]) of vast importance for his immediate successors Greene, Shakspere, Jonson, Marston, and Webster. But of tantamount significance for the drama was the fact, that Machiavelli had been brought on the stage as the incarna- tion of villainy.

Ward says: "The interest taken in Macchiavelli by

---

[1]) This last remark should be carefully noted. The English drama- tists had the whole of so-called Machiavellism before them in the historical figures of King John, Henry IV, and Richard III. Shakspere meant exactly what he said when he made his Richard not the pupil but the school-master of Machiavelli, ("I'll .... set the murderous Machiavel to school"). It was from just such rulers that the Florentine drew his doctrines.

[2]) Cf. Ulrici. „Sein Tamburlaine z. B. athmet in allen Zügen jene Machiavellistische Welt- und Lebensansicht, welche nach Greene's An- deutungen Marlowe getheilt zu haben scheint: ein völlig maassloses Ringen unbeschränkter, despotischer Macht und Herrschaft, dem jedes Mittel zum Zweck gerecht ist, bildet die Basis der Action, wird als das des Mannes allein würdige Streben immer wieder gepriesen, beseelt nicht nur den Helden des Stücks, sondern auch alle seine Gegner und Ge- nossen, und führt daher nur zu einem wüsten Kampfe, der beständig sich erneuert, bis die grössere Macht Tamburlaines alle seine Feinde zu Boden geschlagen hat. Und noch entschiedener, wenn auch nach einer anderen Richtung hin, tritt dieser Machiavellismus in seinem „Juden von Malta" hervor; hier spricht es Marlowe im Prolog (den er Machia- velli in den Mund legt) selber aus, dass diese Lebensansicht die Basis sei, auf welcher das Stück stehe." Sh. Jahrb. I, 62.

English writers was curiously great, if we may judge from the numerous references made to him and his writings, in and out of season. Doubtless it had been fed by the publication in English (in 1537) of the *Vindication* (see Harleian Miscellany, Vol. I)."[1] Any one, even slightly acquainted with English philology, must see that the language of this vindication points to a date of composition at least one hundred years later than Ward accepts. To be sure, the letter purports to be a translation of an epistle written by Machiavelli April 1st 1537 (sic! ten years after his death). In short, it was a notable forgery of the year 1675 appearing at the end of Nevile's translation[2] of Machiavelli's works, and separately in 1688.[3] Nevile says, the letter came into England through "a certain Gentleman", and speaks of Machiavelli as still living in 1537.[4] Farneworth[5] in 1762 declared this letter a forgery; Warburton[6] did the same and all critics since. In fact, it has never been accepted by any authority, nor is it to be found in any Italian edition of Machiavelli's works. As has been seen, Machiavelli was utterly unknown in England up to about 1560; but the historian of "English Dramatic Liteture" had not observed this fact!

---

[1] Ward I, 185.

[2] "The Works of the Famous Nicholas Machiavel ... Translated into English [by Henry Nevile] London 1675" [again 1680, 1694, 1720].

[3] "The Publisher or Translator (i. e. Henry Nevile) of Nicholas Machiavel's whole works .... into English concerning the following Letter of Nicholas Machiavel's wherein he clears himself of the aspersions alledg'd by some on his writings .... Written by the author April 1st 1537. 1688" [again 1691, 1744]. Brit. Mus. Cat. under Machiavelli 8009. a. 19. remarks: "The letter is supposititious; it was written by Henry Nevile."

[4] "We find in the Story of those times that in the month of August following, in the same year 1537, this Nicolo Machiavelli did" — op. cit. Pref. to Reader.

[5] Works of N. M. I, 3.

[6] Cf. Wilson's Works (Dram. of Rest.) 283.

Of Machiavelianism, in the Elizabethan sense of the word, there is not a trace in Tamburlaine: he is all lion, as Techelles says: —

"As princely lions, when they rouse themselves,
Stretching their paws, and threatening herds of beasts,
So in his armour looketh Tamburlaine."

But the "Jew of Malta" is just the opposite: he is all fox. The latter play was the most popular [1]) of all of Marlowe, and constructed for popular sympathy: Barabas, "a true Machiavel", was drawn from popular prejudice based upon Gentillet and not from Marlowe's own study. [2]) The idea of the prologue, as has been said, was a reminiscence of Harvey's epigram; but no happier idea was ever thought of than this for the opening of a tragedy. [3])

"Albeit the world think Machiavel is dead,
Yet was his soul but flown beyond the Alps;
And, now the Guise is dead, is come from France,
To view this land, and frolic with his friends.
To some perhaps my name is odious;   [5
But such as love me, guard me from their tongues,
And let them know that I am Machiavel,
And weigh not men, and therefore not men's words.
Admir'd I am of those that hate me most:
Though some speak openly against my' books,   [10

---

[1]) As Wagner points out, it was played according to Henslowe's diary (ed. Collier) 36 times while Tamb. I, Tamb. II, Massacre, and Faustus were performed in the same time but 15, 7, 9 and 25 times respectively. Cf. "Jew of Malta", ed. Wagner VII.

[2]) In 1810 appeared a characteristic edition. "The Famous Historical Tragedy of the Rich Jew of Malta .... Imitated from the Works of Machiavelli by Christopher Marlo .... London etc." As Wagner remarks "Imitated from the Works of Mach." are original to this edition.   Wagner op. cit. X.

[3]) "Macchiavell's Eingangsprolog wird vorneweg, wie ein Vergrösserungs-Hohlspiegel, aufgestellt, worin die Figur des Juden in kolossalen, aber ebendeswegen, hinsichtlich des specifisch-nationalen Judencharakters, in nebelhaften Umrissen erscheint."
                                        Klein, Gesch. d. Dram. XIII, 676.

Yet will they read me, and thereby attain
To Peter's chair; and, when they cast me off,
Are poison'd by my climbing followers.
I count religion but a childish toy,
And hold there is no sin but ignorance.   [15
Birds of the air will tell of murders past!
I am asham'd to hear such fooleries.
Many will talk of title to a crown:
What right had Caesar to the empery?
Might first made kings, and laws where then most sure [20
When, like the Draco's they were writ in blood.
Hence comes it that a strong-built citadel
Commands much more than letters can import:
Which maxim had [but] Phalaris observ'd,
H'ad never bellow'd in a brazen bull,   [25
Of great ones' envy: o'the poor petty wights
Let me be envied and not pitied.
But whither am I bound? I come not, I,
To read a lecture here in Britain,
But to present the tragedy of a Jew,   [30
Who smiles to see how full his bags are cramm'd;
Which money was not got without my means.
I crave but this, — grace him as he deserves,
And let him not be entertain'd the worse
Because he favours me."   Ed. Dyce 145.   [35

The first four lines show Marlowe thought Machiavelli
had come to England from France; and such was the case,
through Gentillet as Patericke had said. Careful scruti-
nation will find but two thoughts in this whole passage
which come from Machiavelli; and even those at second-
hand. Lines 14 and 15 reflect the general tone of "Principe" 18, but savour more of Gentillet II, 1. Machiavel
speaks of citadels in Prin. 20; Gentillet in III, 33: the
passage 22—23 probably came from the latter. In line 13
is the poison idea, fathered upon Machiavelli by Harvey,
of whom line 19 is also a reminiscence.[1]) Verses 20 and

---

[1]) Ante 18.

21 sound "Machiavellian", [1]) but come from Plutarch, whom
the dramatists seem often to have confounded with the
Florentine.

In the play itself there is not a single line taken
directly from Machiavelli; [2]) and even such passages as
may, directly or indirectly, have been suggested by him,
are so distorted as to present as great a caricature of the
Florentine, as Barabas is of a man. [3])

Since Barabas [4]) was the first pronounced "Machiavel",

---

[1]) I. e. what was and is popularly termed so; they are in reality
diametrically opposed to Machiavelli's teachings. Lee, who studied the
Florentine (cf. Dedication to "Lucius Junius Brutus") carefully for his
"Caesar Borgia" has him thus close the bloody tragedy: —

"No Power is safe, nor no Religion good,
Whose Principles of Growth are laid in Blood." V, 3.

[2]) To be sure, Klein says all is "Von Rechts- und Staatswegen
laut Vorschrift und Gebot der Fürsten- und Staatenbibel, des Principe
von Macchiavell" op. cit. 687. But this is one of the many cases where
Klein's imagination got the better of him.

[3]) "Im "Juden von Malta" tritt Machiavelli als Prolog auf, um
anzukündigen, dass der Jude ein Vertreter seiner Politik sei, der auch
Herzog Guise im "Massacre von Paris" sich ergeben habe. Aber die
wilden Thaten von Marlowe's Helden dienen nicht wie Machiavelli's
Politik einem edeln idealen Endzwecke. Wie Marlowe selbst im Leben,
lassen seine Helden auch in der Dichtung ihre Titanenkraft austoben;
ihre Bethätigung ist sich selber Zweck. Sie alle kennen nur ein
"Wollen". Es tritt ihnen kein Schicksal entgegen wie in der alten
Tragödie, noch ein ethisches "Sollen" wie in der neueren."

Koch: Shak. 246.

[4]) "Der grossartige Prolog des Machiavels kennzeichnet den
Charakter des Helden."

O. Fischer "Zur Char. der Dram. M's." 4.

Honigmann ("Ueber den Char. des Shylocks" Jahrb. XVII, 211)
calls Barabas "ein Vertreter des greulichsten Macchiavellismus"; this is
as absurd as his next remark — "Er zeigt an keiner Stelle irgend
einen jüdischen Charakterzug." Cf. Rabbi Philipson: "The Jew in Eng.
Fiction." p. 26. Elze had already observed that this Machiavellianism
existed only in the poet: "In des Dichters Augen ist diese unerhörte
Verbrecher-Laufbahn nichts als praktischer Macchiavellismus." "Zum
Kaufm. von Ven." Jahrb. VI, 184.

it is necessary to consider his character. To use his own words is the best method.

"As for myself, I walk abroad o' nights,
And kill sick people groaning under walls:
Sometimes I go about and poison wells;
And now and then, to cherish Christian thieves,
I am content to lose some of my crowns,
That I may, walking in my gallery,
See 'em go pinion'd along by my door.
Being young, I studied physic, and began
To practise first upon the Italian;
There I enrich'd the priests with burials,
And always kept the sexton's arms in ure
With digging graves and ringing dead men's knells;
And, after that, was I an engineer,
And in the wars 'twixt France and Germany,
Under pretence of helping Charles the Fifth,
Slew friend and enemy with my stratagems:
Then, after that, I was an usurer,
And with extorting, cozening, forfeiting,
And tricks belonging unto brokery,
I fill'd the gaols with bankrupts in a year,
And with young orphans planted hospitals;
And every moon made some or other mad,
And now and then one hang himself for grief,
Pinning upon his breast a long great scroll
How I with interest tormented him.
But mark how I am blest for plaguing them; —
I have as much coin as will buy the town."   II, 157.

A more incarnate fiend could hardly be imagined. [1])

---

[1]) "The famous Tragedie of the Rich Jew of Malta" hat zu ihrer Basis, wie der Dichter im Prolog selbst andeutet, den vollendeten Macchiavellismus, eine Lebensansicht, welche das menschliche Dasein auf die äusserste Spitze des Egoismus stellt. Der mächtige Trieb nach Selbsterhaltung, nach Glückseligkeit, Macht und Reichthum, tritt in Kampf gegen die ganze Welt; die menschliche Natur ist gespalten, jenes Eine Urelement derselben, ausgeartet in eine rachsüchtige Vernichtungswuth gegen die ganze Menschheit, ist losgerissen von allen übrigen Trieben und Kräften. So steht der Jude da . . . . von leidenschaftlicher Selbstsucht beseelt . . . . Aber auch der Gouverneur und

He is a murderer: only once openly; since he prefers secret
poisoning.[1] When injured he never forgets it: —

> "I am not of the tribe of Levi, I,
> That can so soon forget an injury."   II, 155.

but bides his time: —

> "No, Abigail; things past recovery
> Are hardly cur'd with exclamations:
> Be silent daughter; sufferance breeds ease,
> And time may yield us an occasion,
> Which on the sudden cannot serve the turn."   I, 151.

and seeks deadly revenge.[2] This idea of an injury never
forgot probably came from Gentillet III, 6.[3]
He believes all Christians[4] deceivers: —

> „For I can see no fruits in all their faith,
> But malice, falsehood, and excessive pride,
> Which methinks fits not their profession."   I, 147.

> "Ay. policy! that's their profession,
> And not simplicity, as they suggest." —   I, 150.

Selim Calymath, Christen wie Muhamedaner, handeln in gleichem
schonungslosen Egoismus. Dieser treibt sich im Juden bis zu einer
Höhe, auf der er nothwendig sich selbst vernichtet." Ulrici: Sh. Dram.
Kunst. I, 192.

[1] He strangles Friar Bernardine, and kills by poison his own
daughter, all the nuns, and later Bellamira, Ithamore, and Pilia Borza.
He leads Lodowick and Mathias to death; also Friar Jacomo etc. etc.

[2] When Ferneze takes his goods, he immediately decides upon
killing his son: —
> "So sure shall he and Don Mathias die:
> His father was my chiefest enemy."   II, 158.
When Jacomo converts Abigail: —
> „One turn'd my daughter, therefore he shall die."   IV, 167.

[3] Cf. ante 24 note 2.

[4] When they would take his goods for inherent sin, he cries:
> "What, bring you Scripture to confirm you wrongs?"   I, 149.
It is generally assumed this suggested Shakspere's famous: „The
Devil can cite Scripture" etc.

The main thought of this is to be found in Gentillet II, 1.[1]

He believes himself justified in deceiving them in return: —

> "It's no sin to deceive a Christian;
> For they themselves hold it a principle,
> Faith is not to be held with heretics:
> But all are heretics that are not Jews." II, 159.[2]

He is a consummate dissembler,[3] and believes religion a cloak for crime: —

> "She has confess'd, and we are both undone,
> My bosom inmate! but I must dissemble. —
>
> [Aside to Ithamore.
> O holy friars, the burden of my sins
> Lie heavy on my soul! then pray you, tell me,
> Is't not too late now to turn Christian?" IV, 166.

> "Ay, daughter; for religion
> Hides many mischiefs from suspicion.
>
> — — — —
>
> As good dissemble that thou never mean'st,
> As first mean truth and then dissemble it:
> A counterfeit profession is better
> Than unseen hypocrisy." I, 151.

This, of course, is Gentillet II, 1 and "Principe" 18. He considers treachery a kingly trade: —

> "Why, is not this
> A kingly kind of trade, to purchase towns
> By treachery, and sell 'em by deceit?" V, 177.[4]

---

[1] Cf. also Discorsi II, 2. Prin. 18 — character of Alex. VI.
[2] Cf. II Tamb.
> "— for with such infidels,
> In whom no faith nor true religion rests,
> We are not bound to those accomplishments
> The holy laws of Christendom enjoin:" II, 49.
[3] The Jews call him "good Barabas" I, 148.
[4] This again is a perversion of Prin. 18. Cf. Disc. I, 9 (42): Ist. Fior. VII (193).

He is a perfect egoist: —

> "*Ego mihimet sum semper proximus :*"   I, 148.
> "For, so I live, perish may all the world!"   V, 177.

This is the very gist of Machiavelli's teachings. He is also most subtle and far-seeing: —

> "No, Barabas is borne to better chance,
> And fram'd of finer mould than common men,
> That measure nought but by the present time.
> A reaching thought will search his deepest wits,
> And cast with cunning for the time to come;
> For evils are apt to happen every day."   I, 151.[1])

He has a shrewd insight into politics: —

> "Thus hast thou gotten, by thy policy,
> No simple place, no small authority:
> I now am governor of Malta; true, —
> But Malta hates me, and, in hating me,
> My life's in danger; and what boots it thee,   [5
> Poor Barabas, to be the governor,
> Whenas thy life shall be at their command?
> No, Barabas, this must be look'd into;
> And, since by wrong thou gott'st authority,
> Maintain it bravely by firm policy;   [10
> At least, unprofitably lose it not;
> For he that liveth in authority,
> And neither gets him friends nor fills his bags,
> Lives like the ass that Aesop speaketh of,
> That labours with a load of bread and wine,   [15
> And leaves it off to snap on thistle-tops:
> But Barabas will be more circumspect.
> Begin betimes; Occasion's bald behind:
> Slip not thine opportunity, for fear too late
> Thou seek'st for much, but canst not compass it." —   [20
> V, 175.

Ward [2]) says this speech "has something like the true ring of the *Principe* itself, by which Macchiavelli's name was

---

[1]) Mach. advocates this in Prin. 3. Vide ante 27, note 1.
[2]) I, 186.

chiefly known to the foreign world." Indeed, lines 4, 5
are adopted from Machiavelli; [1]) as also 9—10, and 18—20.
But lines 11—13 show plainly the influence of Gentillet,
and may be compared with:

> "Thus, loving neither, will I live by both,
> Making a profit of my policy;
> And he ,from whom my most advantage comes,
> Shall be my friend." V, 176.[2])

Again; he knows: —

> "And crowns come either by succession,
> Or urg'd by force; and nothing violent,
> Oft have I heard tell, can be permanent." I, 147.

This is the argument of "Principe" II. As the main
drift of "Principe" 18 may be considered: —

> "Be rul'd by me, for in extremity
> We ought to make bar of no policy." I, 151.

He even believes that to follow the dictates of conscience means beggary: —

> „Haply some hapless man hath conscience,
> And for his conscience lives in beggary." I, 147.[3])

He would have his accomplice as himself, void of love,
hope, fear, and pity: —

> "First, be thou void of these affections,
> Compassion, love, vain hope, and heartless fear;

---

[1]) Prin. XVII.
[2]) This as well as the line in the prologue, — "Which money
was not got without my means," can only come from Gentillet's usury-
accusation; for in Machiavelli it is not. Money is Barabas' very soul: —
> "For, whilst I live, here lives my soul's sole hope,
> And, when I die, here shall my spirit walk" II, 153.
He believes it to be the source of all esteem: —
> "Or who is honour'd now but for his wealth" I, 147.
He declares himself: —
> "— a covetous wretch,
> That would for lucre's sake have sold my soul." IV, 166.
[3]) This will be found again in Barnes' "Divels Charter".

> Be mov'd at nothing, see thou pity none,
> But to thyself smile when the Christian moan." II, 157.

He tells the audience he learned his art in Florence — from Machiavelli, of course:

> "We Jews can fawn like spaniels when we please;
> And when we grin we bite; yet are our looks
> As innocent and harmless as a lamb's.
> I learn'd in Florence how to kiss my hand,
> Heave up my shoulders when they call me dog,
> And duck as low as any bare-foot friar." II, 155.[1])

When preparing the poison for Abigail, he refers to Borgia's[2]) wine with the intent to call up in the audience's imagination Machiavelli, popularly supposed to have been Cesare's councillor:

> "Stay; first let me stir it, Ithamore.

> — — — —

> And with her let it work like Borgia's wine,
> Whereof his sire the Pope was poisoned." III, 164.

His scheme of killing all the Turks at a banquet is that described in the "Principe" as used by Oliverotto da Fermo.

He dies blaspheming as Machiavelli was supposed to have done: —

> "Damn'd Christian dogs, and Turkish infidels!
> But now begins the extremity of heat
> To pinch me with intolerable pangs:
> Die, life! fly, soul; tongue, curse thy fill, and die!" V, 178.

Finally, Ithamore declares ~~her~~ his acts under the devil's control; which became the popular opinion concerning Machiavelli: —

> "Why, the devil invented a challenge, my master writ it, and
> I carried it —" III, 162.

---

[1]) Not a word of all this in Machiavelli.

[2]) As with Borgia, it was death to dine with Barabas.
— "Please you dine with me, sir – and you shall be most heartily poisoned." [aside] IV, 171.

Surely, after viewing this demoniac picture of the first Machiavellian,[1]) we shall not wonder at discovering the Florentine conceived by the English dramatists as the very devil incarnate, nor find it strange that Barabas became a stockfigure! No better example could be given of the influence of this play, than, anticipating a little, by citing the case of Heywood, who edited the "Jew of Malta" in 1633, and wrote in the court prologue: — [2])

> "— you shall find him still,
> In all his projects, a sound Machiavill;
> And that's his character."   Dyce 142.

[1]) Cf. Sat. Rev. (Mar. 8, 1884) "The received view, which finds expression both in Shakspere and Marlowe, may have been an exaggerated one, but it is not wonderful that for upwards of two centuries the word "Machiavellian" should have retained the sort of evil connotation which Goethe has since taught us to affix to Mephistophelian." How about Marlowe! also Nation (Oct. 22, 1891): "Machiavelli's Prince has had no peer in modern literature except Goethe's Mephistopheles ..., of course, Machiavelli no more invented the traits which are called by his name than Goethe invented those traits in human nature which he personified in Mephistopheles."

[2]) "Marlowe's Jew of Malta-Tragödie stellt eine solche gegenseitige Durchdringung von geldsüchtigem, mammonischem Juden- und Staatsgeist dar, von jüdischer Geldteufelbesessenheit und Politik. Eine Tragödie, deren Held ein von dämonischer Geldleidenschaft und Gewinnsucht durchglühter Jude-Macchiavell, doch nur als Symbol und Reflex gleichsam des wahren Helden der Tragödie erscheint, der da ist der Staat-Jude; der Macchiavell-Jude, ein Macchiavellischer Principe-Giudeo, die Quintessenz von Macchiavell's Staatsdoctrin; der principielle Eigennutz als Herrschaftgrundsatz, die systematisirte absolute Selbstsucht als Staatsraison, die codificirte Raubsucht, sub specie der absoluten Geld-Anhäufungsgier, und diese in Gestalt eines Juden; unersättliche Geldsucht als eingefleischter Jude. der aber Fleisch von Macchiavelli's Staatsraison ist, der Goldbrünstige, von unbedingter, fanatischer Ausbeutungsgier verzerrte und entbrannte Jude. Fürwahr eine ebenso grossartige, wie von tiefer Erfassung der Solidarität des Juden- und Staats-Macchiavellismus zeugende Geschichtsanschauung; in Rücksicht auf die tragische Bühne von epochemachender Conceptionsursprünglichkeit."   Klein: op. cit. 670.

Cf. also Quar. Rev. Oct. 1885 p. 363.

Up to this time he had never mentioned Machiavelli
in any of his numerous plays; but so vividly had this picture
of Marlowe's been impressed upon his mind, that his very
next play, "A Mayden-Head Well Lost" contains this
passage:

(Stroza in Florence fearing the Prince knows Julia's
past exclaims.)

> "All goes not well, This iugling will be found,
> Then where am I? would I were safe in *Millaine*.
> Here Matchiuell thou wast hatcht: Could not the same
> Planet inspire this pate of mine with some
> Rare stratagem, worthy a lasting character."
>
> (ed. 1874: IV, 146).

and contains such maxims as: —

> "Let millions fall, so I bee crown'd with rest." IV, 151.

Immediately after Marlowe's play in the same year, the
first instance is to be found of a man nick-named Machiavel.

> "You know that Waldegrave's printing presse and
> Letters were takken away . . . . sawen and hewed
> in pieces . . . his Letters melted . . . (by John Wolfe,
> alias Machivill, Beadle of the Stacioners, and most
> tormenting executioner of Waldegrave's goods)." [1]

In this year also appeared a third edition of Whitehorne's "Arte of Warre". [2]

(1589)

Marlowe's call upon Machiavelli was answered by a
host of writers. In the year after (1589) Nashe published

"Tamburlaine became the prototype of the stage hero. Barrabas
became the prototype of the stage villain. To enumerate the characters
modelled on these creations of Marlowe would be to transcribe the
leading *dramatis personae* of at least two thirds of the heroic dramas
in vogue during the latter years of the 16 century."

[1] "Oh read over D. John Bridges" 1588 ed. 1842 p. 30. Herbert
[1170] says, Woolfe was in special favour with the court of assistants,
and chosen from his diligence in hunting out and giving intelligence
of books disorderly printed: this gives point to the sobriquet.

[2] Herbert, II, 784.

Meyer, Machiavelli.

his pamphlet: "The Return of the Renowned Cavaliero Pasquill". In it occurs the following: —

> "How odious and how dangerous innovations of Religion are, Secretarie Machiavell, a pollitick not much, affected to any Religion, discloseth by the example of Fryer Savanaroll." Ed. Grosart I, 103.

This he may have had from the "Principe"; but more likely from Gentillet who discourses much more at large on Savonarola: the words, "Machiavell, a pollitick not much affected to any Religion", certainly come from Gentillet. [1]) In "Martin's Month's Mind" Nashe used *Machiavellists* as a well understood word; [2]) in it we find: —

> "Item, I bequeath to my, lay brethren, my works of Machiavell, with my marginall notes and scholies thereupon; wishing them to peruse, and mark them well, being the very Thalmud, and Alcoran of all our Martinisme." Death and Buriall of Martin Marprelate. I, 191.

As will be seen, the words, "with my marginall notes", are of importance for Greene.

Further on in the same occurs this passage: —

> "Or have you not given him (quoth *Martin the Medium*) an *Italian figge? no no Matt.* That's a Machivillian tricke; and, some of your mates are better acquainted with it." (Op. cit. 174.)

which shows plainly, poisoning was now looked upon as a Machiavellian trick, thanks to Barabas and Gentillet. Again is found: —

---

[1]) Vide Patericke "But it is no mervaile if this Atheist, who hath no religion doth play with Religions deriding all, willing also to persuade a prince to forge a new one" etc. 135.

[2]) "And this is the short summe of Martin's schoole. I meddle not here with the *Anabaptists, Famely Lovists, Machiavellistes,* nor Atheists .... they are so generally scattered throughout every forme." Nashe ed. Grosart I, 164.

"A Machevilian tricke of the Martinists yet in practice.

Againe (which worse was) manie of them [the Queen's Counsellors] I slandered against mine owne knowledge: and I thought it enough, if I might but devise against them the vilest things of the world, to bring them in hatred with the credulous multitude: (a divelish tricke, my sonnes, which I learned in Machivell, but take heede of it, for it asketh vengeance)." Ibid. 182.

This he may have had direct from the "Principe"; but it is also in Gentillet III, 11, and was cited by Father Parsons. [1]) Again occurs the "Machiavellistes"; [2]) the second stanza of "The Author's Epitaph" runs thus: —

> "O! vos Martinistae
> Et vos Brounistae
> Et Famililovistae,
> Et Anabaptistae,
> Et Omnes sectistae
> Et Machivelistae
> Et Atheistae,
> Quorum dux fuit iste
> Lugete singuli." ibid. 199.

and "Young Martin's Epitaph" contains these lines: —

> "*By nature an* Atheist
> *By arte a* Machivelist,
> *In summe a* Sathainist." ibid. 204.

In this year also Shakspere probably produced "Titus Andronicus", a direct outcome of the "Spanish Tragedy"

---

[1]) Ante 24.
[2]) *"Lament ye fooles, ye vices make your moane,*
Yee Ribaulds, *railers, and yee lying lads:*
Yee Scismatiques, and Sectaries, each one:
Yee Malcontents, *and eke ye* mutinous swads:
Ye Machivelists, Atheists, and each mischievous head:
Bewaile, for Martin, your great Captaine's dead." Ibid. 198.

and the "Jew of Malta"; but of the former far more than
of the latter:[1]) Aaron portrays himself, just as Barabas
does, in a passage palpably imitated:[2])

> "Even now I curse the day — and yet, I think,
> Few come within the compass of my curse —
> Wherein I did not some notorious ill:
> As kill a man, or else devise his death;
> Ravish a maid, or plot the way to do it;
> Accuse some innocent, and forswear myself;
> Set deadly enmity between two friends;
> Make poor men's cattle break their necks;
> Set fire on barns and hay-stacks in the night
> And bid the owners quench them with their tears.
> Oft have I digg'd up dead men from their graves,
> And set them upright at their dear friends' doors,
> Even when their sorrows almost were forgot;
> And on their skins, as on the bark of trees,
> Have with my knife carved in Roman letters
> 'Let not your sorrow die, though I am dead.'
> Tut I have done a thousand dreadful things
> As willingly as one would kill a fly;
> And nothing grieves me heartily indeed,
> But that I cannot do ten thousand more.
>
> — — — — — — — —
>
> If there be devils, would I were a devil." V, 1 (125).

Like Barabas he is ever for revenge.

> "Vengeance is in my heart, death in my hand,
> Blood and revenge are hammering in my head." II, 3 (37).

His lust is as characteristic of him, as usury was of
Barabas. He dies blaspheming as Barabas did, and as
Machiavelli was supposed to have done. But this is the
only "Florentine" trait[3]) in him: he does not use poison, nor

---

[1]) Andronicus = Jeronimo: Lucius = Horatio: Aaron = Barabas.
[2]) Vide ante 33.
[3]) Characteristic of all the Elizabethan Machiavellians: it is strange
the dramatists never got hold of Machiavelli's remarkable vision on his
death-bed (vide Blackwood's Mag. II, 691).

has he knowledge of state-matters as Barabas: in short, he is a villain but no "Matchavillain".

(1590)

The next year (1590), in a work of Richard Harvey,[1]) we find Gentillet supposed so well known to English readers that he need be referred to not by name, but simply as "a religious french protestant".

"Italy, in old times the true mirrour of virtue and manhood, of late yeares hath beene noted, to breed up infinite Atheists, such Caesar Borgia was, that using or abusing himself in his life to contemne religion, despised it on his death-bed, ... but of chiefest name those three notable pernitious fellow'es, *Pomponatius* a great philosopher, *Aretine* a great courtier or rather courtisan, *the grandsire of all false and martinish courtiership,* and *Machiavel* a great politicke..... But *Aretine* spake ill of that heavenly God he knew not, and perished through his owne carnall corruption. . . . . Yet Machiavel not so ill *as Aretine,* yet *Machiavel* too ill, God knoweth. This unchristian master of policie, raising up Nicolaites now of his stamp, as Nicholas an Apostata did among the seven Deacons, is not afraid in a heathenish and tyrranical spirit, *l* 2. of warly art, in the person of Fabricio, to accuse the gospel of Christ, and the humilitie of the lamb of God, for the decay of the most flourishing and prosperous estate of the Roman Empire, which fell by its owne idleness and follie, as himself confesseth *l.* 7 . . . . His discoursive accusation is in many mens hands, and I would to God the intended effect. of the discourse were not in some men's harts: howbeit, the same is learnedly confuted, not only by a religious french protestant

[1]) "A Theological Discourse of the Lamb of God and his Enemies. 1590."

whose commentaries are extant, written *ex professo*,
against Machiavel and his anti-christian groundes
of government, ... it is most certaine, that no
man is more carefull to do his dutie, then a christian
conscience . . . . and that secretary of hell, not only
of Florence, is forced to confesse in some places *l*. 1.
disc. c. 11. upon *Livy*, and elsewhere, but most em-
phatically in his proeme to *L. Philip Strozza*, by
vehement and zealous interrogation: *In whom ought
there to be more feare of God, then in a warriour, which
everyday committing himselfe to infinite perils hath most
neede of his helpe?* A right Italian sentence, a notable
word, a fit preserve against the other venims which
this Spider gathered out of old philosophers and
heathen authors; for that it is the wit and disposition of our reformative age, to gather precepts
from those things which our fore-fathers in their
learning judged no better then objections, and to
study those matters for practice, which were first
tought them for their safety, by knowing and
avoiding them —." Op. cit. 94—98.

The author had evidently studied not only Machiavelli
carefully, but also Gentillet, from whom he adopted the
atheism accusation, and that of "having borrowed out of
heathen authors", which as we have seen was the Frenchman's hobby.

In this same year Nashe again refers to the "Prince",
and quotes from it.[1])

---

[1]) "I compared him (Savanarolla) with *Martin* for hys factious head,
pleading in Florence-as Martin did in England, for a newe government,
at such a time as Armes and invasion clattered about their eares. It
may be I am of some better sente then you take me for, and finding
a Machivillian tricke in this plot of innovation, I was the more willing
to lay Savanarol's example before your eyes, that having recourse unto
Machiavell in whom it is recorded, you might see *Machiavel's* judgement upon the same. His opinion is, that when such a peaze may be

In Marlowe's next play, "King Edward II", the character of Mortimer shows the influence of Machiavellian study, though but slightly. He uses Lightborn [1]) to kill the King, and then has him murdered: [2]) Marlowe pictures him as cloaking his villainy under religious hypocrisy, which trait is not to be found in Fabyan, the source of this play.

> "They thrust upon me the protectorship,
> And sue to me for that that I desire;
> While at the council-table, grave enough,
> And not unlike a bashful puritan,
> First I complain of imbecility,
> Saying it is *onus quam gravissimum*;
> Till, being interrupted by my friends,
> *Suscepi* that *provinciam*, as they term it
> And, to conclude, I am Protector now." Dyce 218.

Two other ideas go more directly to the "Principe": —

Mort.) "The king must die, or Mortimer goes down;
The commons now begin to pity him." 217. [3])

Mort.) "Fear'd am I more than lov'd: — let me be fear'd,
And, when I frown, make all the court look pale." [4])

---

drawn through the noses of the people as to beare a change, the Maisters of the Faction are most happie; they may doe what they lust without controlment." "The First Parte of Pasquils apologie." I, 218.

[1]) Lightborn himself must have struck the popular mind as a great Machiavel: he knew even more ways of killing than Barabas.
"I learn'd in Naples how to poison flowers;
To strangle with a lawn thrust down the throat;
To pierce the wind-pipe with a needle's point;
Or, whilst one is asleep, to take a quill,
And blow a little powder in his ears;
Or, open his mouth, and pour quick-silver down.
But yet I have a braver way than these." Dyce 217.

[2]) This is as old as cunning; but, as we have seen, Lorenzo used it: Machiavelli tacitly recommends it in Cesare Borgia. *Ante* p. 26.

[3]) Cf. Prin. XIX: Ist. Fior. VI (85).

[4]) The most notorious of the maxims. Prin. XVII: Gent. III, 9; also Disc. III, 21 (380): Ist. Fior. II (130).

Having heard from the prologue of the "Jew of Malta" that Machiavelli's spirit had once taken up habitation in the Guise,[1]) we would naturally expect to find a disciple of his in the "Massacre at Paris;" but, although he is a murderer, dissembler, and poisoner, there is no Machiavellian feature in this mutilated play except the Guise's hypocrisy in religion.

> "Religion! *O Diabole!*
> Fie, I'am asham'd, however that I seem,
> To think a word of such a simple sound,
> Of so great matter should be made the ground."
>
> Dyce 228.

Shakspere was the next dramatist to mention Machiavelli: *viz.* in I Henry. VI.

> Pucelle) "You are deceiv'd; my child is none of his: [Charles']
> It was Alençon that enjoy'd my love.
> York) Alençon that notorious Machiavel![2])
> It dies, an if it had a thousand lives." V, 4 (72).

Pope took the line, "Alençon — Machiavel", out of the text, and put it in the margin.[3])

Delius remarks here: "Machiavell, als der sprichwörtliche Typus eines schlauen und gewissenlosen Ränkeschmieds, wird hier eben so anachronistisch angeführt, wie in K. Henry VI Third Part .... Sh. kannte ihn vielleicht aus dem Prolog zu Marlowe's Jew of Malta, den der italienische Staatsmann spricht und mit einer Charakteristik seiner selbst eröffnet."[4])

---

[1]) Collier ("Eng. Dram. Poet." II, 512) for this reason, placed the "Massacre" anterior to the "Jew of M.".

[2]) Machevile F. 1, 2, 3. Matchevile F. 4.

[3]) Sh. ed. Clarke-Wright Vol. 5 p. 95. Cf. John.-Steev.-Reed edition Vol. 13 p. 169.

[4]) Sh. ed. Delius I, 849. Cf. Singer-Lloyd Vol. 6, p. 110. "The character of Machiavel seems to have made so very deep an impression on the dramatic writers of this age, that he is many times introduced without regard to anachronism."

But Schlegel's observation on the passage in 3 Henry VI applies here as well as there. . "Einen Anachronismus möchte ich es nicht einmal nennen, wenn Richard der Dritte von Macchiavell spricht. Dieser Name wird hier ganz sprichwörtlich genommen: der Inhalt des Buches vom Fürsten war von jeher vorhanden, seit es Tyrannen gab: Macchiavell hat ihn nur zuerst aufgeschrieben." [1]) It is no more an anachronism to use Machiavelli's name before his birth, than to use "Assassin" in the same way which would appear anachronistic to no one. Schlegel gives us the gist of the whole matter: Shakspere and his contemporaries, like Corneille [2]) and his, simply dubbed all the horrors and cruelties invented by themselves for their tyrant heroes, "Machiavellism"; and for this very reason their use of the Florentine seems to us unskilful and clumsy. [3]) Up to the point where Shakspere [4]) mentions Machiavelli, Alençon has

---

Steevens had already said: "The character of Machiavel seems to have made so very deep an impression on the dramatick writers of this age that he is many times as prematurely spoken of." So, in "The Valiant Welshman", 1615 — (ed. J.-S.-R. XIII, 169).

[1]) "Vorl. über dram. Kunst." II, 180.

[2]) Schlegel says of "Cinna": „Es offenbart sich hier schon die Anlage zu einem Macchiavellismus der Triebfedern, worein die Dichtung des Corneille späterhin ganz und gar ausartete, und der nicht blofs widerwärtig, sondern obendrein meistens ungeschickt und schwerfällig ist. Er schmeichelte sich, in Absicht auf Welt- und Menschenkenntnis, Hof und Politik, die Feinsten zu übersehen. Mit einem grundehrlichen Gemüt hatte er die Anmafsung, „den mörderischen Macchiavell in die Lehre" nehmen zu wollen, und kramt Alles, was er sich von dergleichen Künsten gemerkt hat, breit und lehrhaft aus." ibidem 77. This is exactly what the Elizabethans were doing. It is interesting to compare Lessing also on Corneille. „Die Cleopatra des Corneille, die so eine Frau ist, die ihren Ehrgeiz, ihren beleidigten Stolz zu befriedigen sich alle Verbrechen erlaubt, die mit nichts als mit Macchiavellischen Maximen um sich wirft, ist ein Ungeheuer ihres Geschlechts und Medea ist gegen ihr tugendhaft und liebenswürdig." Hamb. Dram. 11. Aug. 1767.

[3]) The same is true of Ben Jonson's and Alfieri's use of Tacitus. Cf. Schlegel I, 359.

[4]) This essay assumes the three Henry VI to be Shakspere's; if,

shown no Machiavellism; but his very next remark contains
a maxim from the "Principe" or Gentillet, as if to uphold
the sobriquet just given him.

> Alen) "To say the truth, it is your policy
> To save your subjects from such massacre
> And ruthless slaughters as are daily seen
> By our proceeding in hostility;
> And therefore take this compact of a truce,
> Although you break it when your pleasure serves."[1])
>
> V, 4 (159).

That Shakspere had Gentillet in mind is perfectly
evident: the French protestant dedicated his work to Alençon,
and received ridicule in return from the notorious Machiavellian. Shakspere saw the absurdity of this and dubbed
his Alençon "a notorious Machiavel". Not of course, that
it is for a moment conjectured he confounded the two
generations.

(1591)

In the year 1591 Greene, having let Machiavelli rest
since 1583, again used the new-coined word.

> „Sith then this cursed crue, these Machiavilians [cony-
> catchers] that neither care for God nor devill, but
> set with the Epicures gaine, and ease, their *summum
> bonum*, cannot be called to anie honest course of
> living" etc. [2])

---

however, this one is to be attributed to Marlowe, Greene or Peele, in its
original form, surely the vile caricature of Joan d'Arc cries out for
Peele. She is portrayed with the same malignant prejudice which Peele
applied to Longshank's noble wife Eleanor in his "Edward I" to curry
popular applause in defaming Spain, just as has here been done in
traducing France.

[1]) But this is common enough in Shakspere; so in 3 Henry VI.

Edw.) "But for a kingdom any oath may be broken:
I would break a thousand oaths to reign one year."

I, 2 (16).

Cf. Prin. XVIII: Ist. Fior. VIII, (225): also Gent. III, 21.

[2]) "The Second Part of Connie Catching." Grosart X, 73.

As a direct outcome of Marlowe's prologue, must be
• viewed a play called "Machiavel", [1]) now acted at the Rose
theatre. No copy has as yet been found; it was probably
something in the Barabas line. [2])

The next mention of Machiavelli is again made by
Shakspere in "3 Henry VI". He substituted "the murderous
Machiavel" for "the aspiring Catalin" of "The True Tragedy
of Richard III", which he was remodeling. Gloster's monologue
in the "True Tragedy" III, 2 contains just thirty lines.
Shakspere expanded this to seventy-two. Since Shakspere
portrays his Richard as the schoolmaster of Machiavelli, the
parallel passages are given.

Glo.) True Tragedy III, 2 (Delius 933).	3 Henry VI, III, 2 (Delius 963).
"Tut I can smile, and murder when I smile,	"Why, I can smile, and murder while I smile,
I crie content, to that that greeves me most.	And cry, content, to that which grieves my heart,
I can add colours to the Camelion,	And wet my cheeks with artificial tears,
And for a need change shapes with Proteus,	And frame my face to all occasions.
And set the aspiring Catalin to schoole.	I'll drown more sailors than the mermaid shall,
Can I do this, and cannot get the crowne?	I'll slay more gazers than the basilisk;
Tush were it ten times higher, Ile put it downe.	I'll play the orator as well as Nestor,

---

[1]) "Machiavel: A play acted at the Rose Theatre in 1591" Hazlitt
Man. 146.

[2]) That the Machiavel inspired only hatred may be seen from
what Geneste (I, 493) says of a post-Restoration actor:
"Sandford was an excellent actor in disagreeable characters,
such as Creon, Malignii, Jago, and Machiavel [perhaps in
Lee's "Caesar Borgia"] .... Cibber had often lamented that
Sandford's masterly performance was not rewarded with that
applause, which inferior actors met with, merely because they
stood in more amiable characters .... in this disagreeable
light stood Sandford as an actor — from parts he played,
disliked by the multitude." —

Deceive more slily than Ulysses
    could,
And like a Sinon, take another
    Troy.
I can add colours to the Chame-
    leon,
Change shapes with Proteus for
    advantages,
And set the mur'drous Machiavel [1])
    to school.
Can I do this, and cannot get a
    crown?
Tut! were it further off, I'll pluck
    it down.
            III, 2 (182).

Pope put this "Machiavel" line also in the margin; Warburton [2]) wanted to replace "the aspiring Cataline". [3])

Shakspere has made Richard much more of a villain; he is a murderer and a dissembler; he is also quick for revenge: —

"Tears then for babes; blows and revenge for me!" II, 1 (86).

and believes in taking time by the fore-lock.

"Come Warwick, take the time — — — —
Nay, when? strike now, or else the iron cools." V, 1 (47).

---

[1]) Machevill F. 1, 2, 3. — Matchevil F. 4.

Collier remarks: "In the time of Shakespeare, the name of Machiavel had become almost synonymous with a wily, unscrupulous politician. Notwithstanding the anachronism, he therefore substituted "murderous· Machiavel" for "aspiring Cataline" as it stands in "The True Tragedy" 1595,· because he thought the allusion would be better understood." (Sh. ed. Coll. IV, 167). Cf. Athenaeum July 29, 82.

[2]) "And set the mur'drous Machiavel to school." As this is an anachronism, and the old quarto reads: "And set *the aspiring Cataline* to school" I don't know why it should be preferred." Warburton.

Steevens remarks: — "This is not the first proof I have met with, that Shakspeare, in his attempts to familiarize ideas, has diminished their propriety." Sh. ed. John-Steev-Reed 14, 116.

[3]) Malone says in his dissertation: — "Cataline was a person that

He is a supreme egoist:

"I have no brother, I am like no brother;
And this word "love", which greybeards call divine,
Be resident in men like one another
And not in me: I am myself alone". V, 6 (80).

All of this we have had before in Barabas: there is
not a line in the three parts of Henry VI which testifies
to other knowledge of Machiavelli than the mere name,
unless it be the one maxim of perjury [1]) —:

Edw.) "But for a kingdom any oath may be broken:
I would break a thousand oaths to reign one year." (I, 2, 16).

and this one bears the stamp of Gentillet, not of the
"Principe": [2]) or it may have been found in Plutarch, beside

---

would naturally occur to Peele or Greene, as the most splendid *classical*
example of inordinate ambition; but Shakspeare, who was more conversant with English books, substituted Machiavel, whose name was in
such frequent use in his time that it became a specific term for a consummate politician; and accordingly he makes his host in *The Merry
Wives of Windsor*, when he means to boast of his own shrewdness,
exclaim, 'am I subtle? am I a Machiavel?' " Sh. ed. J. S. R. Vol. 14.
Cf. also ed. Collier 4 (167).

The Singer-Lloyd ed. remarks —: "by 'the aspiring Cataline' the
anachronism is also avoided. Machiavel is mentioned in various books
of the poet's age as the great exemplar of profound politicians. An
amusing instance of the odium attached to his name is to be found in
Gill's Logonomia Anglica, 1621: — "Et ne semper Sidneios loquamur,
audi epilogum fabulae quam docuit Boreali dialecto poeta, titulumque
fuit reus Machivellus:

Machil iz hanged And brenned iz his buks Though Machil
is hanged Yet he is not wranged, The Di'el haz him
fanged In his cruked cluks."

The editor should have acknowledged this "amusing instance"
from Boswell (Sh. Mal. ed. Bos. XVIII), where two more lines are
added: — "Machil iz hanged And brenned iz his buks."

[1]) Vide ante p. 58. Cf. also "Malone by Bos." XVIII, 18.

[2]) To be sure, Brandl says — „aber die Wege, welche York wählt,
sind krumm und dunkel. Maulwurfartig wühlt er unter der Erde, in

the very passage, which Greene acknowledged as the source
of one of his most pronounced "Machiavellian maxims".[1])
   Peele also wrote, probably at this time, his "Battle of
Alcazar", in which the moor, Muly Muhamet forms the
connecting link between Barabas and Eleazar in "Lusts
Dominion": Muly is a wretched villain; one who can: —

> "— submit himself and live below,
> Make show of friendship, promise, vow, and swear,
> Till by the virtue of his fair pretence
>
> — — — —
>
> He makes himself possessor of such fruits
> As grow upon such great advantages." II, 3 (Dyce 428).

He cites no maxims, however, but dies cursing as all
these tyrants do.

(1592)

The next year (1592) Marlowe and Shakspere's planting
brought forth a rich harvest. Nicholas Breton opened his
popular citations from Machiavelli.

> "Now, on the left hande, went another crue,
> A hatefull sort, of hellish company:
> Which, to their welth, and wortheless honor grue,

---

den Massen. Ein Schmied verräth uns zuerst seine Umtriebe. Die
Kenter stachelt er zum Aufstand und giebt ihnen an Jack Cade einen
Führer. Er thut jetzt weit Ärgeres als die Chronisten ihm zuschreiben.
Er läfst sich nach Irland schicken, um ein Heer zu sammeln und dann
gegen den Monarchen zu führen, entläfst es aber, da er sich noch zu
schwach fühlt, und spielt den Demütigen, bis ihm königlicher Wort-
bruch erlaubt, mit einem lauten, edel klingenden Pathos dem Hofe
offen entgegenzutreten und zu siegen. Marlowe, Greene, Shakspere
citiert Macchiavelli; die Potentaten der Zeit übertrugen seine rück-
sichtslosen antikisierenden Machtlehren in die Wirklichkeit; sein Typus
des Eroberers aus eigener Kraft — als des einzigen der sich auf die
Dauer halten kann — ward in Marlowes Tamerlan gleichsam verkörpert,
und wie ein Studienkopf aus derselben Schule nimmt sich York aus."
Shak. 63. But this head is eminently Marlowesque and not Machiavellian.
   [1]) "Children", he [Lysander] said, "were to be cheated with cockalls,
and men with oaths." Plut. ed. Langhorne 310.

By wicked workes, of wofull villainy:
Which, by the trades of Machavile instructed,
Were by the devill, to his hel conducted."
Pilgrimage to Paradise. Gros. I, 17.

This is from Barabas; since Machiavelli nowhere instructs how to obtain wealth.

Gabriel Harvey also continues. [1]) Of more importance is the fact that Greene cites him in his most finished and probably last play, "James IV".

Slipper has stolen Ateukin's warrant for Dorothea's murder, and given it to Sir Bertram: —

> Ateu.) "Where be my writings I put in my pocket last night?
> And.) Which, sir? Your Annotations upon Machiavel.
> Ateu.) No Sir." III, 2 (Dyce 204).

The idea of "annotations upon Machiavel", certainly goes back to the phrase of Greene's intimate acquaintance Nashe [2]) „my works of Machiavell, with my marginal notes and scholies thereupon".

Ateukin is, however, a very weak villain; to be sure, he is called a fox, [3]) lives by "cozening the king", [4]) and counsels him to kill Dorothea; [5]) but as soon as his plans go wrong he shows himself a repentant coward. [6]) He lives by

---

[1]) "*Plutarch* is gravely wise; and *Macchiavell* subtilly politike; but in either of them what sounder, or finer piece of cunning, than to reape commodity by him that seeketh my displeasure."
"Foure Letters and Certain Sonnets." Gros. I, 166.

[2]) Vide ante p. 42. 50.

[3]) "Peace, Ida, I perceive the fox at hand." II, 197.

[4]) And.) "My master lives by cozening the king." IV, 208.

[5]) II, 202.

[6]) "O, what are subtle means to climb on high,
When every fall swarms with exceeding shame?

— — — —

O cursed race of men, that traffic guile,

— — · — —

Asham'd of life, asham'd that I have err'd,
I'll hide myself." V, 3 (214).

flattery, [1]) does not deal in poisons, but professes to be an astrologer [2]) and to use charms. [3]) The only Machiavellian counsels he gives are.

> 1. "Why, prince, it is no murder in a king,
> To end another's life to save his own:
> For you are not as common people be
> Who die and perish with a few men's tears;
> But if you fail, the state doth whole default,
> The realm is rent in twain in such a loss.
> 'Tis policy, my liege, in every state,
> To cut off members that disturb the head:" IV, 5 (210).

This is as old in English drama as "Tancred and Ghismunda", and from Seneca, no doubt, though Greene may have been thinking of the Florentine.
Again: —

> 2. "You are the king, the state depends on you;
> Your will is law." [4]) I, 1 (192).

but this is very general. Thus, we see, Ateukin seeking to gratify the king's lust and his own ambition, is not a Marlowesque villain, but one in the future style of Beaumont and Fletcher, more usually entrusted with a royal "liaison" than with „ragioni degli stati".

Greene's play "Alphonsus" is a very palpable imitation of "Tamburlaine." Alphonsus' treatment of Belinus is not unlike Tamburlaine's manner of dealing with Cusroe; — but this Machiavellianism is, of course, at second hand and common enough in all history.

"Selimus", (whether by Greene or not), is another open

---

[1]) His original name appears to have been Gnatho: Cf. 200, 202; also Creizenach: "Anglia" 8, 422.

[2]) I, 1 (191).

[3]) I, 1 (192).

[4]) In this same passage the king is called "a lion" by this "fox", which sounds Machiavellian, but which Greene had from Lysander. Vide "Selimus".

imitation of Marlowe's great Scythian; but contains some
real Machiavellian passages. Selimus is Tamburlaine with
a little of Barabas added to him: he wades to the crown
through blood, and then kills all his helpers; but he uses
poisons, assassins, and such contrivances which Tamburlaine
did not. He exclaims: —

> "Let them view in me
> The perfect picture of right tyrannie." Grosart. 14, 203.

He is a religious hypocrite: —

> "I count it sacriledge, for to be holy
> Or reverence this thread-bare name of good;
>
> — — — —
>
> And scorne religion; it disgraces man." (202)

> "For nothing is more hurtfull to a Prince
> Then to be scrupulous and religious." (258).

All this we have had before in the Guise: incontinently
upon the last passage follows: —

> "I like *Lysander's* counsell passing well;
> If that I cannot speed with lyon's force,,
> To cloath my complots in a foxe's skin."
>
> — — — —
>
> "And one of these shall still maintaine,
> Or foxe's skin, or lion's rending pawes." 258.

which shows Greene had Plutarch in mind. [1])
Selimus knows: —

> "Wisdome commands to follow tide and winde,
> And catch the front of swift occasion
> Before she be too quickly overgone." 202.

This we have also had in Gloucester, as well as in
Barabas.

---

[1]) "When he [Lysander] was told, it did not become the descen-
dants of Hercules to adopt such artful expedients, he turned it off
with a jest, and said "Where the lion's skin falls short, it must be
eked out with the fox's"." Plut. ed. Langh. 309.

Meyer, Machiavelli.

One of his counsellors tells him: —

"He knowes not how to sway the kingly mace
That loves to be great in his peoples grace:
The surest ground for kings to build upon,
Is to be fear'd and curst of everyone.
What though the world of nations me hate? .
Hate is peculiar to a princes state." 245.

This is "the better be feared than loved" maxim already met with, linked to two ideas, which Machiavelli expressly forbids: disrespect of people, and hate, which fear does not necessarily imply. [1])

In this year Greene died a drunkard's death, and left behind him the famous "Groatsworth of wit". In it he attributes to his father, Machiavellian egoism: —

— — "he had this Philosophie written in a ring, *Tu tibi cura*, [2]) which precept he curiously observed, being in selfe-love so religious, as he held it no point of charitie to part with anything, of which he living might make use." Gros. 12 (104).

His dying advice to Lucanio is: —

"Stand not on conscience in causes of profit: but heape treasure upon treasure, [3]) for the time of neede: yet seeme to be devout, else shalt thou be held vile .... what though they tell of conscience (as a number will talke) looke but into the dealings of the world, and thou shalt see it is but idle words ....
See'st thou not daily forgeries, perjuries, oppressions, rackings of the poore, raysing of rents, inhauncing of duties, even by them that should be all conscience, if they meant as they speake: but Lucanio if thou reade well this booke, (and with that he reacht him Machiavel's works at large) thou shalt see what it

---

[1]) Prin. XVII: Ist. Fior. II (130).
[2]) Cf. Barabas *Ego mihimet sum semper proximus.*
[3]) This sounds as if it came from Barabas own lips.

is to be foole-holy, as to make scruple of conscience,
where profit presents itself." Gros. 12 (108).

This whole passage was inspired by Marlowe: Machiavelli never counsels for pecuniary profit. Gorinius, after
handing Machiavelli's works to Lucanio, gives him these
precepts, gathered presumably from the same.

"Make spoyle of yong gallants by insinuating thyselfe
amongst them, and be not moved to think their Aun-
cestors were famous, but consider thine were obscure."

"Regarde not beautie, it is but a baite to entice
thy neighbors eie: and the most faire are commonly
most fond."

"Use not too many familiars, for few proove friends,
and as easy it is to weigh the wind, as to dive into
the thoughts of worldly glosers." [1]

"I tell thee Lucanio . . . . yet saw I never him,
that I esteemed as my friend but gold."[2]

"Love none but thyself if thou wilt live esteemed."
(109).

And all this from Machiavelli!! Further on is the much
mooted passage:

"Wonder not (for with thee wil I first begin) thou
famous gracer of Tragedians, that *Greene*, who hath
said with thee like the foole in his heart, There is
no God, should now give glorie unto his greatnesse: . . . .
Why should thy excellent wit, his gift, be so blinded,
that thou shouldst give no glory to the giver? Is
it pestilent Machivilian pollicie that thou hast
studied? O punish follie! What are his rules but

---

[1] Cf. Prin. XXIII.
[2] Everyone will remember Byron's: —
  "Alas! how deeply painful is all payment!
  Take lives, take wifes, take aught except men's purses,
  As Machiavel shows those in purple raiment,
  Such is the shortest way to general curses" etc.
    Don Juan X, 79.

meere confused mockeries, able to extirpate in a small time, the generation of mankinde. For if *Sic volo, sic jubeo*, hold in those that are able to command: and it be lawful *Fas Et nefas* to doe anything that is beneficiall, onely Tyrants should possesse the earth, and they striving to exceed in tyranny, should each to other be a slaughter man; till the mightiest outliving all, one stroke were left for Death, that in one age man's life should ende. The brocher of this Diabolicall Atheisme is dead, and in his life had never the felicitie he aimed at, but as he began in craft, lived in feare, and ended in dispaire, *Quam inscrutabilia sunt Dei judicia?* This murderer of many brethren, had his conscience seared like Caine; this betrayer of him that gave his life for him, inherited the portion of *Judas*: this Apostata perished as ill as *Julian*: And wilt thou my friend be his Disciple. Looke unto me, by him perswaded to that libertie, and thou shalt finde it an infernall bondage." 142.

All commentators have had their say on this passage. After Storozhenko's carefull examination of all the arguments on the question, little remains but to give his results. Malone [1]) followed by Dyce, Bernhardi, and all critics up to 1874, thought the brocher [broacher] of this Diabolicall Atheisme referred to Kett. Simpson [2]) first insisted upon the reference being meant for Machiavelli, which is perfectly apparent. The Russian professor proves Kett was not at

---

[1]) He probably got his idea from Davies (Athen. Brit. 376—7), who classes Hamont, Lewes, Kett (burned at Norwich 1583, 1579, 1589. Bloomfield: Hist. of Norfolk III, 290) and Marlowe together as upholders of Arianism.

[2]) He says Malone's idea — „is nonsense. The broacher of the Machiavellian doctrine was Machiavelli, who in Greene's day was generally believed in England to have perished by his own hand". Academy: Mar. 21st 1874. The words from, "who in Greene's day etc.", are spoken at random without the least authority.

college when Marlowe was, [1]) and cites Pole, Giovius, Lerois, Ribadeneira, Primaudaye, and Mersenne to prove Machiavelli's supposed atheisme; he might better have referred to Gentillet, who lay much nearer the early Elizabethan dramatists, and is never tired of denouncing the Florentine as an atheist.

How utterly false this accusation was, readers of Machiavelli know; he was anything but an atheist, [2]) though he dared to compare heathenism with Christianity. So much then for Greene, who followed in the footsteps of Marlowe [3]) (in ascribing *auri sacra fames* to Machiavelli's teachings), and Gentillet (in denouncing him as an atheist). To this he added his own damnable forgery, that Machiavelli died cowardly by his own hand, as Judas was supposed to have done. Simpson had absolutely no authority for his statement that "in Greene's day Machiavelli was generally believed in England to have perished like Judas by his own hand"; this was Greene's own foul fabrication. But what more was to be expected from this blaggard liar, puking forth his putrid surfeit from a drunkard's death-bed!

The next dramatist to mention Machiavelli was Nashe in this same year. Thus in "Summer's Last Will and Testament": —

Winter) "Nay I will justify, there is no vice
    Which learning and vile knowledge brought not in,
    Or in whose praise some learned have not wrote.
    The art of murder Machiavel hath penn'd;

---

[1]) Cf. Athen. Cant. II, 38.

[2]) Cf. Discorsi I, 11. Byron's own note to "Childe Harold" IV, 54.
„Here Machiavelli's earth return'd to whence it rose"
is interesting: — „The fact is, that Machiavelli, as is usual with those against whom no crime can be proved, was suspected of and charged with atheism."

[3]) As Simpson (Sh. Allus. Books I, XLVIII) says: "Marlowe was really as much opposed to Machiavelli's reputed teachings as Greene himself —".

Whoredom hath Ovid to uphold her throne,
And Aretine of late in Italy,
Whose Cortigiana teacheth bawds their trade.
Gluttony Epicurus doth defend.   Dod.-Haz. [1]) 8 (72).

The passage explains itself, and can refer only to the "Prince". [2])

Now also appeared Nashe's "Pierce Penniless's Supplication to the Devil", and in it the following:

"There is no friendship to be had with him that is resolute to doo or suffer anything rather than to endure the destinie where to he was borne; for he will not spare his own father or brother to make himselfe a gentleman. France, Italy, and Spain are full of these false-hearted Machivillians"; Shak. Soc. 12 (24).

This idea of not sparing anyone "to make himselfe a gentleman" is evidently from Gorinius advice in Greene's "Groatesworth" just given. But this is not enough to be fathered upon Machiavelli; we have heard, "The Art of murder Machiavel hath penned", now read what instructions this "Art of Murther" gives.

"O Italie, the academie of manslaughter, the sporting place of murther, the apothecaryshop of poyson for all nations! how many kinds of weapons hast thou invented for malice! Suppose I love a man's wife,

---

[1]) Dodsley compared Orion's lines p. 44.

"That they [dogs] have reason, this I will allege:
They choose those things that are most fit for them,
And shun the contrary all that they may."
with "Dell' Asino d'Oro" VIII

"Questa [hogs] san meglior usar color che sanno
Senz' altra disciplina per se stesso
Seguir lor bene et evitar lor danno."
These two passages are about as similar as "dogs" and "hogs".

[2]) Hazlitt remarks: "This was the popular idea at that time, and long afterwards, of Machiavelli, arising from a misconception of his drift in "Il Principe"."

whose husband yet lives, and cannot enjoy her for his jealous overlooking, phisicke, or, rather, the art of Murther, (as it may be used) will lend one medicine which shall make him away in nature of that disease he is most subject too, whether in the space of a yeare, moneth" — 34. [1])

Then for a finale to this demoniac capriccio: —

„I comprehend . . . . lastly, under hypochrisie, al Machiavilisme, ... outwarde gloasing with a man's enemie, and protesting friendship to him I hate and meane to harme, [2]) all under-hand cloaking of bad actions with common-wealth pretences; [3]) and, finally all Italianate conveyances, as to kill a man and then mourne for him, [4]) *quasi vero* it was not by my consent, to be a slave to him that hath injur'd me, and kisse his feete for opportunities of revenge, [5]) to be severe in punishing offenders, that none might have the benefite of such means but myselfe, [6]) to use men for my purpose and then cast them off, [7]) to seeke his destruction that knows my secrets; [8]) and such as I have employed in any murther or stratagem, to set them privily together by the eares to stab each other mutually, [9]) for fear of bewraying me; or, if that faile, to hire them to humour one another in such courses as may bring them both to the gallowes:" 68.

---

[1]) This kind of poisoning was alluded to in "Leicester's Commonwealth" but not as Machiavellian.
[2]) Barabas and Selim; Guise and Henry; Mortimer and Kent.
[3]) Barabas, Guise, Mortimer.
[4]) Barabas and Barnardine; Mortimer and Edward.
[5]) Barabas and Ferneze.
[6]) Mortimer and Edward.
[7]) Barabas and Jacomo; Mortimer and Lightborne.
[8]) Barabas and Ithamore; Guise and Admiral; Mortimer and Kent.
[9]) Queen-Mother to Henry and Navarre.

As is here done, so might almost all the so-called "Machiavilisme" in Elizabethan literature be traced to Marlowe and Gentillet. What more could be expected, when we find this passage from one of the best Italian scholars among the literati, — from „The English Aretine", who certainly knew Machiavelli in the original!

(1593)

'In the next year (1593) Gabriel Harvey wrote in "A New Letter of Notable Contents" against Nashe for defending Greene: —

> "Aretine was a reprobate ruffian; but even Castilio, and Machiavel, that were not greatly religious in conscience, yet were religious in policie": Gros. I 292.

In "Pierce's Supererogation" Harvey never tires of citing Machiavelli as a catch-word against Nashe; [1]) but he also gives testimony again to knowledge of the "Principe", [2]) of

---

[1]) "Yet would he [Nashe] seeme as fine a Secretary with his pen as ever was Bembus in Latin, Macchiavell in Italian or Guevara in Spanish or Amiot in French." Op. cit. Gros. II, 276. Compare with this such clumsy wit as, —

> "*Apulius Asse* was a pregnant Lucianist ... A golden Asse: *Machiavel's Asse* of the same metall and a deepe Politican like his founder ... He that remembreth the governement of Balaams Asse ... Machiavel's Asse ... little needeth any other Tutor." 248.

and this:

> "Lucian's Asse ... Machiavel's Asse, myself since I was dubbed an asse by the only Monarch [Nashe] of Asses, have found savoury herbs amongst nettles". 292.

and such pointless nonsense as:

> "It was nothing with him to Temporise *in genere*, or *in specie*, according to Macchiavel's grounde of fortunate success in the world; that could so formally, and featly Personise *in individuo*. 299.

[2]) "So Caesar Borgia, the soverein Type of Macchiavel's Prince, won the Dukedom of Urbin, in one day." 306.

the "Discorsi": [1]) he recognizes him as a profound politician,[2])
and praises his style. But still even he cannot keep from
calumniating him in the Elizabethan spirit, using the fact
of his banishment most unfairly.

> "Ferrara could scarcely brooke Menardus a poysonous
> Phisitian .... Florence more hardly tollerate Macchia-
> vel, a poysonous politician: Venice most hardly endure
> Arretine, a poysonous ribald: had they [Greene and
> Nashe] lived in absolute Monarchies they would have
> seemed utterly insupportable." 94.

The comparison of Greene and Nashe to Machiavelli
and Aretine is facetious enough; but here again we see the
influence of Gentillet, who had already denounced the
Florentine as poisonous and as hunted out of his native
city.[3]) His influence is apparent in another passage: —

> "No, Homer not such an authour for Alexander; nor
> Xenophon for Scipio: .... nor Macchiavell for some
> late princes: nor Aretine for some late Curtezans
> as his Authour [Greene] for him [Nashe] the sole
> authour of renowned victorie." 78.

for, "by some late princes" he can only mean the French,
whose great use of Machiavelli he must have known from
the father of "Machiavellisme" — Gentillet.

Harvey, also, brings Plutarch and Machiavelli together
where they were often confounded in the drama:

> "Lysander's Fox, Ulysses' Fox... might learn of him
> [Nashe] ... For Stephen Gardiner's Fox, or Machia-
> vel's Fox are too young cubbes, to compare with
> him." 297..

Nashe again, in his "Christs Teares over Jerusalem",
heaps almost incredible ignominy upon Machiavelli:

---

[1]) "I will not enter in Macchiavel's discourses, Jovius Elogyes" etc.
                                                          — 78.

[2]) "— profound Politiques, like Macchiavell, or Perne —" 307.

[3]) Ante p. 7.

"The worlde woulde count me the most licentiate
loose strayer under heaven, if I should unrippe but
halfe as much of their ["private Stewes"], veneriall
Machavielisme, as I have lookt into. We have not
English words enough to unfold it. Positions and
instructions have they to make their whores a hundred
times more whorish and treacherous, then theyr own
wicked affects (resigned to the devils disposing) can
make them." — Grosart. IX, 231.

Then follows what simply cannot be quoted — and
Machiavelli was the author of this! But here, as in his
other defamations, Nashe was merely following the general
lead, and pandering to popular prejudice; for in an epistle
prefixed to this very book the next year, occur passages
which show a good knowledge of the real Machiavelli![1]) He
also repeats one of the "maximes", already well known to
English readers.

"Henceforth with the forenamed Machiavel, for an
unrefutable principle I will hold it, that he is utterly
undone which seekes by new good turnes to roote
out old grudges." Ibid. 4.

After the mention of Machiavelli in Henry VI (1 and 3),
we may safely conclude, had Shakspere known his works,
he would certainly have used them in portraying Richard III.
Gloucester is a "dreadful minister of hell" — "subtle, false
and treacherous"

Glo.) "The secret mischiefs that I set abroach,
I lay unto the grievous charge of others.

— — — —

But then I sigh, and, with a piece of scripture,

---

[1]) Many courses there be (as Machiavell inspiredly sets downe)
which in themselves seem singular and vertuous, but if a man follow
them they wilbe his utter subversion, others that seeme absurd, odious,
and vitious, that well looked into will breed him most ease." Op. cit. 3.
Cf. Prin. XV.

Tell them, that God bids us do good for evil:
And thus I clothe my naked villainy
With old odd ends stol'n forth of holy writ,
And seem a saint when most I play the devil." [1]) I, 3 (324—).

These two subterfuges are Machiavellian; but we have
already had both in Barabas and in the Guise.

Richard knows,

"that fearful commenting
Is leaden servitor to dull delay.
Delây leads impotent and snail-paced beggary;
Then fiery expedition be my wing,
Jove's Mercury, and herald for a king." IV, 3 (51—).

Machiavelli also lays much emphasis upon rapidity in
decision and action; but this again we have had before in
Barabas.

As Richmond says, he is: —

"One raised in blood, and one in blood establish'd;
One that made means to come by what he hath,
And slaughter'd those that were the means to help him."
                                        V, 3 (247—).

This is eminently Machiavellian; but was also historical,
and well known in the drama. Richard thinks: —

"Conscience is but a word that cowards use."

but Barabas had already scoffed at conscience.

Richard's leading motive is Gentillet's maxim III, 4
(Prin. VII); but this lay nearer Shakspere in his historical
sources. Again Gentillet II, 1 (Prin. XVIII) III 8, (Prin.
XVII) 9, (Prin. XVII) 10, (Prin. XXIII) 11, (Prin. VII) 12,
(Prin. XVIII) 18, (Prin. XVIII) 19, (Prin. XVIII) 21, (Prin.
XVIII) 23, (Prin. XVII) might be cited as eminently dis-
played in Richard; but all of these had already been used
by Marlowe: and all Richard's fierce egoism was in Barabas

---

[1]) Cf. III, 7 "Enter Gloucester aloft, between two Bishops". This
was Buckingham's counsel.

"Ego mihimet sum semper proximus". We can only conclude Shakspere did not know Machiavelli in the original; but drew from Marlowe, [1]) and from history: [2]) that Richard was considered a Machiavellian "par excellence" by Elizabethans, was natural enough after what has been seen of the popular prejudice. [3])

---

[1]) Richard III is the most Marlowesque of all Shakspere's characters. "As with the chief personages of Marlowe's plays, so Richard in this play rather occupies the imagination by audacity and force, than insinuates himself through some subtle solvent, some magic and mystery of art. His character does not grow upon us; from the first it is complete." Dowden: "Sh. Mind and Art". 182.

[2]) Shakspere even diminishes rather than increases, (as is generally supposed), the historical and legendary horrors thrown about Richard by his predecessors and contemporaries. "Wenn hiernach also thatsächlich zwei Holinshed'sche Versionen des Charakters und der Handlungen Richards vorliegen, so hat Shakespeare allerdings die auf More basirte, also die schwärzere, gewählt; über diese ist er aber nicht, wie so vielfach behauptet wird, hinausgegangen, sondern er hat sie sogar gemildert." Oechelhäuser, Jahrb. III, 38.

[3]) To some, this discussion of Richard III will seem very scant: to such as have really studied the great Florentine unprejudiced it must appear all that conservatism can say. Richard III was the school-master of Machiavelli, not the pupil. Cf. Kuno Fischer "Richard III." (86): "Richard könnte ein Vorbild sein für den "principe" des grossen italienischen Staatsmannes; bei ihm könnte ein Machiavelli in die Schule gehen! So gut wusste Shakespeare was er zur Charakteristik Richards mit diesem Namen an dieser Stelle wollte, aus der man häufig nichts weiter herausgefunden hat als den Anachronismus zum Beweise des unwissenden Shakespeare."
Simpson's statement ("Pol. Use of Stage" New Sh. Soc. II, 428) — "he [Rich. III] comes on the stage as the ideal Machiavellian prince" — certainly needs qualification; and that of Gervinus (Shak. II, 108) that Richard was given "Machiavelli schon in Heinrich VI. zum Muster und Meister" is not true. Bleibtreu ("Gesch. der Eng. Lit." 51) adopts Gervinus' view. Schlegel (op. cit. II, 298) hits the nail on the head; Rich. III out-Machiavels the supposed Machiavel. "Er erfüllt sein zuvor gethanes Versprechen, den mörderischen Macchiavel in die Schule zu senden."

(1594)

Greene, as has been shown, following Gentillet accused Machiavelli of atheism, and Marlowe of having adopted it from him. In 1594 appeared the third English edition[1]) of Piere de la Primaudaye's "Academie Françoise": in the "Epistle Dedicatorie" we find: —

"Let Florence testifie this [the spread of atheism] to all posteritie succeeding, where that monster *Machiavel* first beganne to budde, who hath now spreadde abroade his deadly branches of Atheisme over the most countries in Christendome, insomuch as fewe places but are so well acquainted with his doctrine, that the whole course of mens lives almost everywhere, is nothing else but a continual practice of his preceptes." Epis. Ded.

and in the "Epistle to the Reader": —

"In the fore-front of which compaine [of Atheists], the students of *Machiavel's* principles and practicers of his precepts may worthily be ranged. This bad fellowe whose works are no lesse accounted of among his fellowers then were Apollo's Oracles among the Heathen, nay then the sacred Scriptures are among sound Christians, blusheth not to belch out these horrible blasphemies against pure religion, and so against God the Author thereof, namely, *That the religion of the heathen made men stout and courageous, whereas Christian religion maketh the professors thereof base-minded, timerous, and fitte to become a pray to every one; that since men fell from the*

---

[1]) „The French Academie .... By Peter de la Primaudaye .... newly translated into English by T. B. The Third edition 1594." The passage occurs first in this third edition (1 ed. 1586, 2 ed. 1589, 3 ed. 1594, again 1602—5, 1614, 1618) and in all subsequent. It is significant that until Greene's pestilent Machiavellian policy, atheism, became notorious, the translator (Thomas Bedinfeld?) did not deem it necessary to inveigh against it; but he was now caught up in the popular current.

religion of the Heathen, they became so corrupt that they would beleeve neither God nor the Devill: that Moses so possessed the land of Judea, as the Gothes did by strong hand usurpe part of the Roman Empire. These and such like positions are spued out by this hel-hound .... in trueth he would have all religion to be of like accompt with his disciples, except it be so far forth as the pretence and shewe of religion. may serve to set forward and effect their wicked pollicies. And for this cause hee setleth downe this rule for every Prince and Magistrate to frame his religion by, namely, that *he should pretend to be very religious and devout, although it bee but in hypochrisie.* And to this he addeth a second, precept no less impious that *a Prince should with toothe and nail maintaine false myracles and untrueths in religion, so long as his people may thereby be kept in greater obedience."* [1])

Then after inveighing violently against Greene he continues: —

"The voice of a meere Atheist, and so afterwards he pronounced of himselfe when he was checked in conscience by the mightie hand of *God.* And yet this fellowe in his life time and in the middest of his greatest ruffe, had the Presse at commandement to publish his lascivious Pamphlets —"

He then denounces "Stage-plays and Theatres" and ends:—

"Wherefore my humble suit is to all such as may by vertue of their authoritie stay the violent course of Atheisme dayly spread abroad by these pernicions, that they would lay to their helping hand for the speedy redresse thereof." Epis. to Read.

From this we see atheism had become wide spread two

---

[1]) It is almost needless to say that these are from Gentillet II, 1 and 2 verbatim: this whole attack presumes no more knowledge of Machiavelli, than had been obtained from Gentillet's maxims in the second division.

years after Greene's death, that it was now universally attributed to Machiavellian studies, and that as such it was
feared the dramatists and pamphleteers were promulgating it.

In this year also appeared the second edition of Nashe's
"Pierce Penniless". In the letter to the publisher occurred
a significant passage: —

> "Had you not beene so forward in the republishing
> of it, you shold have had certayne epistles to orators
> and poets, to insert to the latter end; as, namely,
> to the ghost of *Machevill* .... to the ghost of *Robert
> Greene*, telling him what a coyle there is with pam-
> phleting on him after his death. They were prepared
> for Pierce Pennilesse first setting forthe, had not the
> feare of infection detained me with my lord in the
> country." Sh. Soc. 12 (XIV).

This shows that immediately after Greene's death he
was associated with Machiavelli. In another pamphlet Nashe
refers again to Machiavellian deceit, [1] and accuses the devil
of having learned a much-used tricke from the Florentine.

> "This Machevillian tricks hath hee [the devil] in him
> worth the noting, that those whom he dare not uni-
> ted or together encounter, disjoined and divided, he
> will one by one assaile in their sleepe." "Terrors of
> Night" Gros. III, 223.

In Shakespere's Richard II, probably of this year, is to
be found: —

> "And that's the wavering commons: for their love
> Lies in their purses, and whoso empties them,
> By so much fills their hearts with deadly hate."
> II, 2 (129 —).

This thought is in the "Principe"; but Shakspere probably observed it for himself. [2]

---

[1] "You that are Machiavelian vaine fooles, and think it no wit
or pollicie but to vowe and protest what you never meane" — "Ter-
rors of the Night". Gros. III, 279.

[2] Cf. Prin. III. Burghley said: "Plebis anglicanae ingenium ad

(1595)

In the next year (1595) W[illiam] C[lerke] repeated almost exactly what the translator of Primaudaye said, and accused Machiavelli of being the instrument of Sathan.[1] Now appeared the first English translation [2]) of the "Storia Fiorentina" by Thomas Bedingfield; probably the same who englished Primaudaye.

---

seditiones praeceps si pensitationibus extra ordinem opprimantur." Cf. Simpson New Sh. Soc. II, 409.

[1]) "Religion's speech: And although I poore Religion am not so good a states man, that willingly I intermeddle with matters of the common wealth, yet I must say thus much in the true defense of my selfe, that since profane Machivell hath obtained so much credit amongst the greatest states men of all Europe, Atheisme hath perswaded the world to my death, and tolde Princes that there was no religion. Can any counsell be more pernicious to the common wealth? more dangerous to a Country? more fatall to a Prince? then onely to relie in causes of greatest importance upon his owne wisdome? to seem to have that religion in shew, which he never meaneth to embrace in trueth? to prefer Heathens before me? to ascribe felicitie to fortune, and not to vertue and true religion? And these with divers others of like impuritie hath that profane Atheist broached into the world, which was no sooner drunke by the states of Europe, but some of their kingdomes have come to ruine ... I dare say thus much, that religious Princes, while confidently in a good cause, they have fullie relied upon God's assistance, they have notablie triumphed over all enemis: thus in the old Testament Abraham, Moses, Josua, Gedeon ... all triumphed over multitudes of their enemies, because I (howsoever contemned by prophane Machivel) was the sole conductor of all their armies: ... But I am loath to rake in the dead cinders of polluted Machivell, whom though Satan made an instrument to disgrace me, and with his dregges dangerouslie poysoned the best states, yet shall my trueth like the sun from under a cloude shine clearely in the days of Elizabeth." "England to her three Daughters." Grosart 106.

[2]) "The Florentine Historie ... Translated into English by T(homas) B(edingfield) Esquire. London 1595." The translator says it was made in 1588; it was dedicated to Hatton, and made no aspersions on Machiavelli, but praised him highly. Vide Sinker: "Cat." 297.

In Shakspere's "King John" Pandolf says to Lewis: —

"A sceptre, snatch'd with an unruly hand,
Must be as boisterously maintained as gained;
And he that stands upon a slippery place,
Makes nice of no vile hold to stay him up:
That John may stand, then Arthur needs must fall;
So be it then, for it cannot be but so." III, 4 (135).

This sounds very Machiavellian in the mouth of the cardinal of Milan, but history speaks here again.

(1596)

The year (1596) following, Nashe closed his long list of Machiavel-citations by using the word, coined from the Florentine's name, as synonymous for deception.

"His [Harvey's] malicious defamation of Doctour *Perne:* when after that he hath polluted him with all the scandal he could, hee saies, The clergie never wanted excellent fortunewrights, and he was one of the chiefest: as though the church of *England* were upheld and Atlassed by corruption, Machiavelisme, apostatisme, hipocrysie." —

Lodge now showed himself quite conversant with Machiavelli's writings: with the Prince, [1]) with the "Dis-

---

[1]) "Sedition . . . This is a pestilent fiend, and the more secret hee lurketh, the more harme he worketh, the whole scope of his discourse is the cause of much inconvenience, for there through on everie side groweth hate, and of hate saith *Machiavell* come divisions, and of divisions sects and of sects ruin." Wits Mis. 67 as below. Cf. Prin. XVII.

"— and though the course of intelligence according to *Machiavell* be necessary in an estate, and worthy the execution of a considerate and good man (for his countries sake) yet the Sparta being laid on his shoulders that hath no honestie, maketh that estate odious, which otherwise would be honest." *Wits Miserie, and the World's Madnesse: Discoursing the Devils Incarnate.* Gosse II, 87.

corsi", [1]) "The Art of War" [2]) and even "Belphegor"; [3]) but
nevertheless he could not keep from falling into the cant use.

> "Among all other the counsellors of this young and
> untowarde heire [Arsadachus] .... there lived a great
> Prince in the court of *Protomachus*, who delighted
> rather to flatter then counsell, to feede corruptions
> then purge them, who had Machevils prince in his
> bosome to give instance." — A Margarite of America
> Gosse I, 22.

and again: —

> The next Harpie of this breed is *Scandale* and
> *Detraction*. This is a right malcontent Devill, You
> shall alwaies find him his hat without a band, his
> hose ungartered, ... he hath read over the coniu-
> ration of *Machiavel*. In beliefe he is an Atheist ....
> hating his countrie .... not for default either in
> governement, or pollicy, but of meere innated and
> corrupt villainie; and vaine desire of Innovation."
> Wits Mis. ibid. 17.

After Ward's careful analysis of the relation of Shylock
to Barabas, little need be said of the direct outgrowth of
the former from the latter. Shakspere's Jew in the" Merchant
of Venice" also suffers what Barabas had "learned in
Florence".

> "Still have I borne it [Antonio's rating] with a patient shrug,
> For sufferance is the badge of all our tribe.
> You call me misbeliever, cut-throat dog,
> And spit upon my Jewish gaberdine,
> And all for use of that which is my own." I, 3 (110)

---

[1]) "Ill would they observe that golden sentence of *Cornelius Tacitus* registered by *Machiavell*, who saith, That men ought to honor things past, and obey the present, desiring and wishing for good Princes, and howsoever they prove to endure them." Ibid. 18. Discorsi III, 6.

[2]) "If (according to Machiavel's doctrine) he [Ambition] have a great State opposed against him." — Ibid. 8.

[3]) The "incarnate devil" of drunkenness is called "Beelphogor". Ibid. 78.

Lancelot says: —

"Certainly the Jew is the very devil incarnal."

but he is more humane than Barabas. [1])

He is also as eager for revenge: — "if it will feed nothing else it will feed my revenge" — and uses religious hypocrisy: —

> "An oath, an oath, I have an oath in heaven:
> Shall I lay perjury upon my soul?
> No, not for Venice." [2]) IV, 1 (228—).

But he neither murders by underhand means, nor dissembles, nor poisons as Barabas does; in short, he is much less even of an Elizabethan Machiavellian. [3]) To the audience, perhaps, his most Florentine trait was his great wealth and covetousness, which idea had been introduced by Marlowe.

(1597)

In the next year (1597) [4]) one of the most popular poets of the day, William Warner, shows that he had become acquainted with Gentillet, and that he knew reference to

---

[1]) Ithamore says he acts under the devil. Ante p. 41.

[2]) Cf. also the famous: — "The devil can cite scripture for his purpose."

[3]) Cf. Elze "Zum Kaufm. von Ven." Jahrb. VI, 185. "Die Rohheit dieses sich in Blut wälzenden und unmögliche Greuel gebärenden Macchiavellismus [in Barabas] hat Sh. glücklicherweise hier wie anderwärts beseitigt. Wie sehr derselbe jedoch nach dem Geschmack des englischen Volkes war, beweist der Umstand, dass nach Sh. Chapman mit Beifall dazu zurückkehren konnte; seine Tragedy of Alphonsus z. B. lässt darin wie auch hinsichtlich des Styls erkennen, dass ihr nicht Sh. sondern Marlowe als Vorbild gedient hat."

[4]) It is significant that the editions of „Albions England" of 1589 (6 bks.) and 1592 (8 bks.) display no reference to Macchiavelli; the edition 1597 (12 bks.) first contains the passages cited and they are in all subsequent editions 1602 (13 bks.) and 1612 (15 bks.) with no additional citation.

Machiavelli would be delectable to his audience. After
calling the counsellor of the Queen-Mother and King
Charles:

> "a politition" —
> "A Germaine (to whose lore),
> Have Machivilian French-events
> Since sorted ever-more"
> Albion's Eng. X, 57 (Chalmers 624).

the author proceeds to paraphrase an entire chapter of
the „Principe",[1]) and concludes: —

"When this, and worse than thus, this worse than Machivel had said,
With that conventicle's applause so working was not staid:

For hence, if accidents we shall observe, may be collected
The civill warres and butcheries in France to have affected."

---

[1]) "He told his travels, and instates his observations: how,
Besides the only Turke, he none a monarch did allow:

Who suffreth none by might, by wealth or blood, to overtop:
Himself gives all preferments, and whom listeth him doth lop.

His bands of Janizaries, who are form'd and nourisht still
From Childhood his own creatures, hold all at his own will.

He out of these his captaines, and his bassies doth elect;
They do deserve their founder's trust, his only weal affect

The rather, for their dignities, and all that all possessé
Determine at his will, behooves therefore not to transgresse.

Save his religion, none is usde, unless in conquests late,
And that of policie, thereby to adde unto his state,
Nor even these permits he of religion to debate.

Nor walled townes, nor fortresses, his empier doth digest;
Except upon the frontiers, for securing of the rest.

His subjects thus, theirs, and the whole, at his devotion needs
No imposts, taxes or the like, whence tumult often breeds.

Discourst of his experience thus, he then descends to it
Whereby of Monarchia might himselfe the French king fit.

"Whereas" (quoth he) French policie consists of three estates,
The princes, nobles, commons, and each one of th'other wates —

This shows plainly enough his knowledge was from French [1]) sources. Later on this characteristic passage occurs: —

"— over-ronne The free Italian states .... as Naples, Millaine
.... to rich-built Genoa goe:
But farre from drifting Florence keep, least Machiavels yee groe."
XII, 75 (648).

Breton again displays the ignorant prejudice of the age in his "Wits Trenchmour".

"Indeed sir quoth the Schollar, hee that doth for other, for I thanke you, tell he say to himselfe I beshrew you, hee may have more kinde wit, then commodious understanding: but by your leave, among

For hearts and helps, and oft the king is bridled of those three,
Himselfe therefore, such lets remov'd, sole monarch thus might bee.

Of ancient peere, of valiant men, great lords, and wisemen all,
By forced warre, or fraudfull peace, to temporize the fall:
Whereto religion's quarrel then presented meane not small.

Meanwhile, untill of them by turnes weare riddance, did behove
To worke them mal-contents, the king to labor vulgar love.

Immediately, even from himselfe, no whit at their request,
To passe preferments, not to them, but els as likes him best:

And but of peeces ruinous the great ones to possesse:
And when his creatures shall grow to more those great to lesse,

To quarrel then those nobles, when in them great hearts would lurk,
That for the souldier, or the sword of justice should make work.

So to provide that of the states be no convention nam'd,
Religion not disputed of: strong townes, which oft have tam'd

The French kings, be dismantled: And when things as thus be fram'd,
His Majestie" (quoth he) "shall hit the marke whereat he aim'd!"
Op. cit. 624—.

This is simply "Principe" IV versified.

[1]) He also accuses Catherine de Medicis of atheism as Gentillet had done.

„And Katherine de Medicis whose atheisme wrought much woe."
X, 58 (627).

many that have been studients in this course of instruction, I finde one notable vile creature, whose philosophy I may rather call mortall than morrall, his notes are so full of poyson, to the spirit of all good disposition: and this good old Gentleman his name was Machavile. Oh quoth the Angler, a vengeance of all villaines, I think there was never such another: he hath left such devillish lessons to the worlde, that I thinke he will hardlie come at heaven. I pray you sir, quoth the Angler, [1]) let me intreate you to recite some of them." Grosart II, 12.

Then the scholar quotes: —

"That it was good for a man of conscience to keep the bands of his oath: and yet when pollicie may purchase a good purse,[2]) an oath hath been ventured for a lesse matter then a million" .... "Fathers in the governement should be feared of theyr Children" .... "That it is good for Maisters to be bountifull to their servants, were it not that Keepers will say, that fatte hounds will hunt but lazilie." .... "That he that will not curtsie to a Milstone, make musick to an Owle, daunce Trenchmour with an Ape, and fall to wonder at a Wethercocke, may hope after nuts, and pick on shells for his comfort."

The angler refutes each in turn and continues: —

„Tush man quoth he, are these of his notes? Not in these wordes, but to this effect aunswered the Schollar."

The scholar then tells of "certaine notes of a scholler of his" [Machiavelli's] in which such villainy is set forth as "to finde out a prodigall heire to use him like a younger brother";[3])

---

[1]) This is good: the angler calls Machiavelli's doctrines "most devillish" and then naïvely asks what they are!

[2]) Here we see influence of Barabas.

[3]) This must go back to Greene's "Groatsworth".

and "if there were ever a lawyer of a large conscience, what a bribe might doo for a conveiance." [1])

The angler calls this "scholler of his", "a pretty scholler at the devill's [Machiavelli's] alphabet". Thus every villainy under the sun was supposed to come from the Florentine. Bacon's essays of this year show that he was aa careful student [2]) of Machiavelli: he stands forth among the Elizabethans as the only man who really knew the Florentine; and he never falls into the cant use of popular prejudice. One example of Bacon's citation will suffice:

"Of Goodnesse and Goodnesse of Nature: *The Italians* have an ungracious proverb: *Tanto buon che val niente*: *So good that he is good for nothing.* And one of the Doctors of *Italy, Nicholas Macciavel,* had the confidence to put in writing, almost in plaine Termes: *That the Christian Faith had given up good Men, in prey to those, that are Tyrannical, and unjust.* Which he spake, because indeed there was never Law, or Sect, or Opinion, did so much magnifie Goodnesse, as the Christian Religion doth." [3]) Essays ed. Wright 48.

In this year appeared a Latin drama "Machiavellus" by D. Wiburne; [4]) but the Florentine's name is merely used to characterize an intriguing servant; knowledge of Machiavelli there is none in the play.

In Shakspere's "Henry IV" Brandl would see in one place the influence of Machiavelli.

"Machiavelli warnt seinen Emporkömmling vor übermässiger Grausamkeit im Gebrauche der gewonnenen

---

[1]) Even the proverbial simony of lawyers imputed to Machiavelli!

[2]) Cf. Kuno Fischer "Franz Baco" 267.

[3]) Cf. "Discorsi" II, 2, also "Of Seditions" — p. 55 — Discorsi III, 27. "Of True Greatnesse — 118 and Prin. 13. "Of Counsell" — 82 and Prin. 22. "Of Vicissitude" — 232 and Discorsi II, 5 etc. etc.

[4]) „*Machiavellus*: a Latin drama by D. Wiburne acted at Cambridge in 1597. There is a copy of it in MS. Douce 234, transcribed in the year 1600." Haz. Manual 146.

Macht. Wir werden später bei Heinrich IV. sehen, wie dieser Usurpator den Wink befolgt und durch eine passende Milde in der That die Herrschaft behält. Richard III vergisst in diesem Punkte seine gewohnte Klugheit." Shak. 70.

One is inclined to ask, did Shakspere observe nothing of the philosophy of history for himself? [1])

(1598)

In the next year (1598) "The Mirrour of Policie" referred to Machiavelli as authority on the government of Venice. [2]) Edward Guilpin made the usual cant citation on hypocrisy.

> "For when great Foelix, passing through the street,
> Vayleth his cap to each one he doth meet

— — — —

> Who would not think him perfect curtesie?
> Or the honey-suckle of humilitie?
> The devill he is as soone: he is the devil
> Brightly accoustred to bemist his evil.

— — — —

> *Signior Machiavell*
> Taught him this mumming trick, with curtesie
> T'entrench himselfe in popularitie."
>
> "Skialetheia": Grosart 36.

---

[1]) If such hair-splitting *Quellenforschung* is to be applied to Shakspere (or other dramatists as well), a thousand and one passages might be traced to Machiavelli or to almost any writer on political history, e. g. Sh. "Ant. and Cleop." III, 1.

Vent.) "Who does i'the wars more than his captain can,
Becomes his captain's captain."

Machiavelli warns a prince, that if an auxiliary general conquer for you, you are his prisoner (Prin. XIII) — but to claim this as Shakspere's source would be absurd.

[2]) "Scarce is the like Commonweale to be found .... by report of Machivile." 17.

Shakspere again made direct mention of Machiavelli, in "The Merry Wives":

> Host) "Peace, I say! hear mine host of the Garter. Am I politic? Am I subtle? Am I a Machiavel? Shall I lose my doctor? no: he gives me the potions and the motions. Shall I lose my parson? my priest? my Sir Hugh? no: .... Boys of art, I have deceived you both." III, 1 (102).

Here, of course, the use is that of a mere catchword, of which the play is full;[1]) but it was a most facetious flash of genial wit to have mine host of the Garter call himself by the Florentine's name.[2])

Ben Jonson now began his citations of Machiavelli, in "The Case is Altered".

> Jun.) "Do you hear, sweet soul, sweet Radamant, sweet Machavel? one word, Melpomene, are you at leisure?" IV, 4 (Gifford-Cunningham II, 542).

Juniper says this when calling out Rachel for Onion. This is the first instance of a woman being called a Machiavel; but he calls her Rhadamant also, and is very careless of the meanings of his strange expressions. As Gifford says "Juniper was .... exceedingly popular" (II, 554.):

---

[1]) So I, 1 "Mephostophilus, Sackerson"; I, 3 "bully Hercules, Caesar, Hector, Sir Pandarus, Lucifer, II, 1 Sir Acteon"; II, 3 "Aesculapius, Galen"; and "Hibbocrates, Doctor Faustuses, Goliath" etc.

It was probably a reminiscence of Marlowe: in later plays Machiavelli, Mephistophilus and Faustus often occur as mere catch-words together.

[2]) "Der schlaue Wirth, ein Grossthuer voll Spott und Streichen, der sich selbst für einen grossen Politiker und Machiavell hält, den der Kitzel sticht jeden zu foppen, vexirt den pedantischen Waliser Evans; er mufs denselben Verdruss haben wie Falstaff, dafs die Einfältigen, die nicht einmal Englisch sprechen können, sich gegen ihn verbinden und den Durchtriebenen um seine Pferde prellen." Gervinus: Shak. II, 286.

this calling Rachel a "Machavel" [1]) is not the least merry
of his meaningless phrases. [2])

Marston took occasion to cite Machiavelli in the popular
manner, [3]) in his second satire: of a puritan hypocrite he
says: —

"— who thinks that this good man
Is a vile, sober, damned politician?

— — — —

---

[1]) If dates are to be considered, this was an anachronism on the
part of the careful Ben; since the comedy plays in Italy during Emperor
Sigismund's († 1437) reign.

[2]) To call a subtle woman a Machiavel became quite a "fad".
Cf. Congreve: "The Double Dealer" II, 6 (Hunt. 181).

Mellefont (believing himself outwitted by Lady Touch-
wood). "So then, spite of my care and my foresight, I am
caught, caught in my security. — Yet this was but a shallow
artifice, unworthy my Machiavelian aunt."

also Farquhar: "The Constant Couple" II 4 (ibid. 522):

Lady Lurewell) "Welcome, my dear sir Harry, I see
you got my directions.

Sir H.) Directions! in the most charming manner, thou
dear Machiavel of intrigue."

also: Colman and Garrick, "The Clandestine Marriage" V, 2 (Mod.
Brit. Dram. IV, 506):

Miss Sterling (to Mrs. Heidelberg of sly little Fanny).
"I had no desire to sleep, and would not undress myself knowing that my Machiavel sister would not rest 'till she had
broke my heart."

also: Murphy: "The Upholsterer" I, 3 (444)

Quidnunc (after his failure — to his daughter Harriet).
"Poh, poh. I tell you I know what I am about — you shall
have my books and pamphlets, and all the manifestoes of the
powers of war.

Har.) And make me a politician, sir!

Quid.) It would be the pride of my heart to find I had
got a politician in petticoats — a female Machiavel! 'S bodi-
kins, you might then know as much as most people they talk
of in coffee-houses."

[3]) As will be seen, Marston obtained later a careful knowledge of
Machiavelli, and held a very high opinion of him.

O is not this a courteous-minded man?
No, foole, no; a damn'd Machiavelian;
Holds candle to the devil for a while,
That he the better may the world beguile,
That's fed with shows." Marston ed. Bullen III, 271 —.

Anthony Munday, who had been in Italy, produced about this time his "Downfall of Robert Earl of Huntington": one passage in which, though it may possibly be a reminiscence of Plutarch's Lysander, savors of the "Principe".

Leicester, tearing off John's usurped royalty: —

"Come off, this crown: this sceptre off!
This crown, this sceptre are King Richard's right;
Bear thou them, Richmond, thou art his true knight.
You would not send his ransom, gentle John;
He's come to fetch it now. Come, wily fox,
Now you are stripp'd out of the lion's case,
What, dare you look the lion in the face?"
IV, 1 (Dodsley VIII, 178).

However this may be, direct reference was made to Machiavelli in another play of this year; *viz.* "Mucedorus". The hero will disguise himself to rescue Amadine, and seeks counsel of Anselmo.

Ans.) "That action craves no counsel,
    Since what you rightly are, will more command,
    Than best usurped shape.
Muc.) Thou still art opposite in disposition;
    A more obscure servile habiliment
    Beseems this enterprize.
Ans.) Then like a Florentine or mountebank!
Muc.) 'Tis much too tedious: I dislike thy judgement,
    My mind is grafted on an humbler stock."
Dodsley VII, 207.

This is the first reference in the drama, supposing Machiavelli so well known as that only his native city need be mentioned; but the same recurs often enough later on.

(1599)

Shakspere's portrait of Richard III had been accepted
as that of a Machiavel: in an hexameter poem "The Pre-
servation of Henry VII" Richard is denounced as such: —

> — "he spared nobody, whose life
> Might dominire for a king, whose life might work him a mischiefe.
> He was a vile Machavile, and still took time at avauntage:
> To work such stratagems his lew'd mind gave him a courage."[1]

— — — —

again,

> "But now, now murtherus horror,
> And Machavile stratagems I recorde, of a lewde malefactor.
> That did usurp as king, that killed his own very brethren,
> Murdered his nephues wife, and mony peeres, on a sudden.

— — — —

> Trewly my minde doth abhorre that I should here make the recitall,
> What Machavile policies, what shifts, what crafty devices,
> What tyranus stratagems he devis'd to crucifie princes." Ibid. 58.

but this is little more than the cant use.[2]

Nashe in this year defending his master, Aretine, took
occasion again to traduce Machiavelli.[3] How familiar he
had become to play-goers, may be seen by looking at "Lust's
Dominion", a palpable imitation of Marlowe and Shakspere.
Eleazar is an amalgamation of Barabas and Aaron, having

---

[1] Collier: "Illustrations of Old English Literature" II, 54. It is
to be hoped these are genuine, though they may be falsifications.

[2] Compare this of Sir Pierce of Exton.

> This trecherus bludy Duke did bring eight tal men in harnesse,
> Each man a bill in his hand, like thieves, to murder his Highnesse;
> Who with a bill that he got by force, did manfuly withstand.
> Those Machavile hipochrites (for he kild foure with his owne hand)"
>
> Ibid. 57.

[3] — „of that treatise *de tribus impostoribus mundi* which was
never contrived without a generall counsell of devils, I am verily perswaded it was none of his [Aretine's] ... Certainly I have heard that
one of *Machivel's* followers and desciples was the author of that
booke," — "The Unfortunate Traveller" ed. Gosse 107.

the villainy of the one, and the lust of the other: he is called "the black prince of Devils"; dying, he exclaims: —

> "Devils, come claim your right, and when I am
> Confin'd within your kingdom, then shall I
> Outact you all in perfect villainy." V, 6 (Dods. XIV, 191).

Where he had conned his super-Satanic devilry, may be seen in this: —

> "Zarack and Balthazar, come hither, see,
> Survey my library. I study, ha,
> Whilst you two sleep: marry 'tis villainy.
> Here's a good book, Zarack, behold it well,
> It's deeply written, for 'twas made in hell;
> Now, Balthazar, a better book for thee;
> But for myself this, this the best of all;
> And therefore do I claim it every day,
> For fear the readers steal the art away." [1]) V, 6 (188).

This book must be the „Principe", as Ward suggests. Eleazar may have studied Machiavelli, but the anonymous author certainly did not; for there is not one passage in this lascivious trash which shows any influence whatever. [2])

We see that Machiavelli was now considered a much greater villain than the personification of all evil: we need not wonder, when it is stated later on, that Nicholas Machiavel gave the devil his sobriquet of "Old Nick".

Ben Jonson again made a popular citation of Machiavelli this year in his "Every Man out of his Humour". In the chorus between acts II and III, Cordatus says to Mitis,

---

[1]) In Aphra Behn's rifacimento "Abdalazar" this is omitted; the point being no longer significant.

[2]) Eleazar goes through the usual stage villainy: he uses poison (II, 6. 131) and religious hypocrisy.
> "sin shines clear,
> When her black face religion's mask doth wear." II, 2 (121).
He also cuts off all his accomplices in crime (Crab, Cole, Queen-Mother, Cardinal etc.), but cites no maxims.

that to judge all courtiers by Fastidious Brisk, or all wives by Deliro's wife: —

— "were to affirm that a man writing of Nero should mean all emperors; or speaking of Machiavel, comprehend all statesmen: or in our Sordido, all farmers; and so the rest." (Giff.-Cuning. 96.)

(1600)

In 1600 Hakluyt makes the cant use of Machiavelli[1] en passant: and Breton links Achitophel and the Florentine together, resuscitating. Gentillet's old thought, that Machiavelli's principles if followed would lead to ruin.

"Hee that is . . .

— — — —

And loves Achitophell for wickednesse

— — — —

He that of Machavile doth take instruction
To manage all the matters of his thought;
And treades the way but to his owne destruction,
Till late Repentance be too dearly bought,
Shall finde it true, that hath beene often taught,
As good be Idle as to goe to schoole,
To come away with nothing but the Foole."

"Pasquils Passion" Gros. I, 25.

About this time appeared "Grim, the Collier of Croydon". As Pegge[2] says, "the story of this play is taken in part from Machiavelli's Belphegor". The dramatist may have had the original. before him, but more likely Riche's version.

In "Patient Grissel" of this year occurs a thought to

---

[1] "Hee [the King of Spain] may bee perswaded, that to leave no other succour or safetie to his nakednesse, but the olde stale practice of . . . hyring and suborning some Machavellian underhande by secret conveyance, to stop the course of our proceedings . . . is but a poore, weake, and uncertaine stay to upholde his estate by." III, 685.

[2] Apud Dodsley VIII, 391. Cf. also Ward II, 138.

be found in the "Principe" [1]); but also in almost every poet since Homer's day.

Gwälter) "But teach your jocund spirits to ply the chase;
For hunting is a sport for emperors."
Shak. Soc. 1841 p. 3.

(1601)

In the next year (1601) Henslowe mentioned in his diary a drama by Day and Haughton, "Friar Rush and the Proud Woman of Anthwerp". Since there is no "proud woman" in the Rush legend, but in Machiavelli's Belphegor, which was often confounded [2]) with the story of the popular necromancer, it may be assumed that this play was a mixture of the two. As Herford says: —

> "It is obvious that this plot [of Belphegor] which can hardly have been unknown to the scholarly and cultured Day, would give point to the title of this last play which on the other hypothesis it does not possess." "Lit. Rel. of Eng. and Ger." 309.

Marston in his "Antonio and Mellida" cited Machiavelli, and was the first dramatist to speak a good word for him.

Antonio is diguised as a fool; besought to put off his masquerade he exclaims: —

> "Why, by the genius of that Florentine,
> Deepe, deepe observing, sound brain'd Macheveil,
> He is not wise that strives not to seem fool
> When will the Duke holde feed Intelligence,
> Keepe warie observation in large pay,
> To dogge a fooles act." [3])
> II. Ant. and. Mell. IV, 1; Halliwell 117.

---

[1]) Cf. Prin. XIV: Arte d. Gu. V (351) Disc. III, 39 (431).
[2]) Herford: 308—318.
[3]) Cf. Piero) "He that's a villain, or but meanly soul'd,
> Must still converse and cling to routs of fools,
> That cannot search the leaks of his defects."

This idea originates in the drama with Marston, and is the leading thought in "The Malcontent".

Piero, in part II, with his awful heaps of villainy and murder, is as typical an Elizabethan Machiavel as Barabas. He uses Strotzo to murder Feliche, and then treacherously strangles him.

> "Why, thus should statesmen doe,
> That cleave through knots of craggy policies,
> Use men like wedges, one strike out another,
> Till by degrees the tough and knarly trunke
> Be riv'd in sunder." IV, 3 (123). [1]

This policy we have had again and again. Incontinently upon this follows a thought perverted from the "Principe".

> Ant.) "Pish! most things that morally adhere to souls,
> Wholly exist in drunk opinion." [2]

Marston seems to have known Machiavelli's writings well, and to have understood them as will be apparent in "Sophonisba". In this same play, part I, Piero, having conquered Genoa from Andrugio, immediately seeks to destroy him and all his kinsmen, [3]

> "Which I'll pursue with such a burning chase,
> Till I have dried up all Andrugio's blood." I, 1.

When seeking Antonio's death, he first has Strotzo defame him [4] by accusing him of having murdered his own father. This is really Machiavellian; but he exclaims: —

> "I am great in blood,
> Unequall'd in revenge." [5] I, 1.

This is clearly the influence of the Barabas-Aaron-

---

[1] *Vide ante.* Span. Trag. p. 26. As Aronstein (Eng. Studien XX, 35) says "Für den zweiten Theil ist die Spanish Tragedy des T. Kyd das wichtigste Vorbild gewesen".
[2] Cf. Prin. XVIII.
[3] This method is advocated in Prin. VIII. Cf. Disc. III, 40 (434).
[4] Cf. Prin. VII, also Gent. III, 2.
[5] He defames his own daughter for revenge.

Eleazar type, also seen in his dissembling, [1]) poisoning, and general villainy, [2]) guided by a devil. [3]) Again Marlowe and Machiavelli are mixed up: —

> "Where only honest deeds to kings are free,
> It is no empire, but a beggary." II, 1.

There can be no doubt that Marston used the "Principe" for this drama; but Marlowe's influence was even stronger than Machiavelli's.

(1602)

In the next year (1602) was published the translation [4]) of Gentillet made by Patericke in 1577: it called forth a host of citations. William Bas continued the cant use. [5]) Breton did the same, [6]) and warned against Machiavel's instructions: —

> "Flie Machivile his vile instructions,
> Which are but poysons to a princely minde:

---

[1]) "And didst thou ever see a Judas kiss
  With a more covert touch of fleering hate?" Pt. II. I, 1.

[2]) "Poison the father [Andrugio], butcher the son [Antonio] and marry the mother [Maria] ha!" Ibid. I, 1.

[3]) Strotzo) "I would have told you, if the incubus
  That rides your bosom would have patience".
                                        Ibid. I, 1.

[4]) Ante p. 15.

[5]) "The merchant, or the Machivilian,
  The Yeoman, tradesman, clowne, or any one,
  What ere he be, we turne our backs to none."
  Sword and Buckler or The Servingman's Defense."
                                        Collier, Illus. II, 13.

[6]) "It [ingratitude] bringeth foorth such shamefull Evill,
  Out of the shamelesse wicked minde;
  As by suggestion of the Divell,
  Makes Nature goe against hir kinde;
  When Men that should bee Vertue's friends,
  Become but Machavilian fiends."
                      Unthankfulnesse. Gros. I, 4.

Meyer, Machiavelli.

— 98 —

And noted well, are but destructions,
That doe the world with wicked humors blinde:
And do the soule to hellish service binde.
Where nothing for gaine must be forbidden,
While divels in the shape of men are hidden."
Mother's Blessing. Gros. I, 8.

Chettle took occasion to traduce Machiavelli very violently in his "Hoffman". Ferdinand, having adopted Hoffman (as Otho in disguise) and disinherited his son the fool Jerome: —

> Jer.) "They say I am a fool, Stilt; but follow me; I'll seek out my notes of Machiavell: they say he is an odd politician.
> Stilt) Ay, faith, he's so odd that he hath driven even honesty from all men's hearts." II, 2 (Lennard 22).

The silly Jerome's [1]) remark is intended, of course, for parody; but Stilt's answer is in earnest, and shows Machiavelli was thought to have driven all honesty from the world. Hoffman is a villain of deepest dye: he employs Lorick in murder and then kills him; he also uses poison, dissimulation, awful revenge etc., etc. in the Elizabethan Machiavellian way, but cites no maxims.

In another play of this year proverbial use is made of the perjury accusation, and there is added to "Machivelisme" an idea, first introduced into the drama by Marlowe. Thus in Dekker and Marston's Satiromastix.

Horace has sworn not to traduce Tucca any more: —

> Tucca) "I know now th'ast a number of these *Quiddits* to binde men to th' peace: 'tis thy fashion to flurt Inke in everie man's face: and then to craule into his bosome, and damne thyself to wip't off again: yet to give out abroad, that he was glad to come to composition with me: I know *Monsieur Machiavell* 'tis one a thy rules; My long-heel'd Troglodite, I could make thine ears burne now, by dropping into them, all those hot oathes, to which, thy selfe gav'st voluntarie fire, (when thou wast the man in the Moone) that thou would'st never squib

---

[1]) Chettle, no doubt, had Greene's Ateukin in mind.

out any new Salt-peter Jestes against honest Tucca, nore those Maligo-tasters, his *Poetasters:* I could Cinocephalus, but I will not, yet thou knowest thou hast broke those oathes in print, my excellent infernal.

Horace) Capten —

Tucca) Nay I smell what breath is to come from thee, thy answer is, that there's no faith to be helde with Heretickes and Infidels, and therefore thou swear'st anie thing": ed. Pearson I, 235.

This maxim, "there's no faith to be held with Heretickes", is taken almost word for word from "The Jew of Malta".[1]) Since Dekker [2]) never makes mention of Machiavelli in his individual dramas and Marston does, this citation may be imputed to the latter. This was the year of two lost plays by Chettle and Heywood: "The London Florentine"[3]) in two parts. "The Florentine" can refer only to Machiavelli; but as to the nature of the play it would be waste time to conjecture.

(1603)

In 1603 John Davies also presumed Machiavelli so well known, that he needed to be referred to only as the Florentine, just as was done in Mucedorus.

"The *Aire* we breath doth beare an Ore herein,
And being subtil moves the simple *Minde;*

---

[1]) Ante p. 35.

[2]) He seems to have made no use of Machiavelli. Langbaine says: "The beginning of "If it be not good the devil is in it" seems to be writ in imitation of Matchivel's novel of Belphegor: where Pluto summons the Devils to Council." *Momus Triumphans* 122.

But Herford shows that Langbaine's supposition, expanded by Halliwell to the assertion that "the principal plot of the play is founded on Belphegor", is absolutely untenable, and the play arose from the Friar Rush legend. (Herford 308—318.) A careful examination of Dekker's play shows it to contain no reminiscence even of Machiavelli.

[3]) Cf. Chettle ed. Lennard XII.

For, never yet was *foole* a *Florentine,*
As by the wise hath well observed byn."
"Microcosmos." Grosart. I, 32.

Henry Crosse fancied Machiavelli especially hurtful to age:[1]) and Breton seemed to be growing tired of all the so-called Machiavellian policies in books.

He dedicates to John Linewray his "Dialogue of Pithe and Pleasure": —

"Wherein it may be you shall finae pleasant wittes speake to some purpose, no Machavilian pollicies, nor yet idle fables", — Grosart II, 4.

The translation of Montaigne's essays mentioned Machiavelli[2]) *en passant*: in the same is also to be found the lion-and-fox maxim:

"Pope Boniface the Eight is reported to have entered into his charge as a Fox, to have carried himself therein as a Lion, and to have died like a Dog." Florio ed. Morley, 165.

That Jonson had read Machiavelli carefully is apparent from the "Discoveries":[3]) we would naturally seek

---

[1]) — "to speake somewhat of those vaine, idle, wanton Pamphlets and lascivious love-books [in Aretine's manner] ... as hurtful to youth, as *Machavile* to age." *Vertus Commonwealth.* Grosart 89.

[2]) "Machiavel's discourses were very solid for the subject, yet hath it been very easie to impugne them, and those that have done have left no lesse a facilitie to impugne them." Florio ed. Morley 336.

[3]) Almost the whole cap. 9 of the Prin. is incorporated in the Discoveries. A fair specimen of their coincidence is e. g. Giff-Cunn. 404: *Nobilium ingenia* and *Principum varia.*

Prin. 9. "E non sia alcuno che ripugni a questa mia opinione con quel proverbio trito che *chi fonda in sul popolo, fonda in sul fango;* perchè quello è vero quando un cittadino privato vi fa sù fondamento, e dassi ad intendere che il popolo lo liberi quando esso fusse oppresso dagl' inimici o dai magistrati." Cf. also Disc. I, 48.

Jon. (*loco cit.*). "Nor let the common proverb (of he that builds on the people builds on dirt) discredit my opinion: for that hath only place where an ambitious and private person, for

his influence in "Sejanus". Several passages contain thoughts
to be found in the Florentine's writings; but since Jonson
never cites them as his authority and always goes back to
Tacitus, Sallust, Livy etc.: it must be concluded, the coin-
cidences[1]) in this "prodigious rhetoric" and Machiavelli arise
in having been drawn from the same sources.

——————

> some popular end, trusts in them against the public justice
> and magistrate."

Again:

> "*Clementia.* — *Machiavell.* — A Prince should exercise his cruelty
> not by himself, but by his ministers; so he may save himself
> and his dignity with his people, by sacrificing those when he
> list, saith the great doctor of state, Machiavell." (405). This
> comes from Prin. 7 — and is refuted by Jonson.

And again: under *Clementia tutela optima* (405) Prin. cap. 8
> is cited and refuted: — "He that is cruel by halves (saith
> the said St. Nicholas) loseth no less the opportunity of his
> cruelty than of his benefits" — When Jonson here canonized
> Machiavelli, he was, no doubt, thinking of the cant term for
> thieves (St. Nicholas' Clerks) so often used in the drama;
> *vide* B. and F. "Loyal Subject" III, 4 (330): Webster "Cure
> for a Cuckold" IV, 1: Wilson "The Cheats" I, 1 (18).

To suppose this idea of Mach. being considered the patron saint
> of pads was meant in earnest, or other than a merry jest,
> would be as absurd as to think Butler was serious in
> saying, "Machiavel gave name to our Old Nick", which
> Macaulay actually seems to have thought. It is interesting
> to compare with Jonson's "St. Machiavel", Lacy's "The Dumb
> Lady" III, 1 (59).

Doctor) "Nurse ... I'll show thee a reverend book, called St.
> Aretine's, where you shall be convinced there's no such thing
> as honesty." Cf. ibid. also V, 1 (94 D. of R. IV).

[1]) *Sej.*) "Whom hatred frights, Let him not dream of sovereign-
ty ... The prince who shames a tyrant's name to bear, Shall never
dare do anything but fear; All the command of sceptres quite doth
perish, If it begin religious thoughts to cherish":
  II, 2 (Giff. Cunn. I, 288). Cf. Prin. XVII: Disc. III, 19 (377).
Tib.) "The prince that feeds great natures, they will sway him
  Who nourisheth a lion, must obey him." —
    III, 3 (304). Cf. Prin. XIII: Disc. II, 20 (254).
Mac.) "He that will thrive in state, he must neglect The trodden

In this year Shakspere produced another fine villain, Angelo in "Measure for Measure": he is more in the manner of Beaumont and Fletcher than of Marlowe. One would hardly call him a Machiavellian; and yet Davenant, in his "Law against Lovers", an amalgamation of this play and "Much Ado", did not hesitate to have Benedick impute his brother Angelo's villainy to Machiavel's books.

> Beatrice)   — "Benedick,
> We will cast off the serious faces of
> Conspirators, and appear to the deputy
> As merry, and as gay, as nature in
> The spring. This house shall be all carnival,
> All masquerade.
> Benedick) Good! we will laugh him [Angelo] out
> Of's politics, till he make paper kites
> Of Machiavel's books, and play with his pages
> In the fields." IV, 1 (Dram. of Rest. V, 168).

(1604)

Next year (1604) appeared a book, the title of which is characteristic of the times, and shows that Ben Jonson's application of the Florentine's name to a woman had not passed unnoticed. It is called, "The Unmasking of a feminine Machiavell" by Thomas Andrew. [1]) From this title something might be expected, but it turns out to be merely a fierce diatribe upon a false woman; this calling a prostitute, a "Machiavel" was probably a reminiscence of Nashe, who had already imputed the art of venery to the Florentine statesman. [2]) One passage is, however, very significant

---

> paths that truth and right respect: And prove new, wilder ways: for virtue there Is not that narrow thing, she is elsewhere; Men's fortune there is virtue; reason their will; Their licence, law; and their observance, skill. Occasion is their foil; conscience, their stain; Profit their lustre; and what else is, vain." III, 3 (305).

[1]) Cf. Drake: "Sh. and his Times" I, 676.

[2]) Ante p. 59.

of what Machiavelli had now become to the popular mind.

"That damned Politician *Machiavell*,
That, some say, had his *Maximes* out of hell, [1])
Had he but beene a schollar unto her,
To learne his Arte, need not have gone so farre.
She of her owne would have imparted store
Of cursed plots, ne're thought upon before,
Such and so deepe, as none could e're devise,
But her great Grandsire, father of all lyes.
With the *Hienaes* voyce can she beguile,
And weepe, but like the *Nile*- bred *Crocodile*,
That on the pray she instantly devoures,
Dissembling teares in great abundant powers.
With the *Cameleon* can she change her hiew,
Like every object that her eye doth view,
Proteus was never half so mutable
As the unconstant, of her word unstable:
Her eyes like *Basilisks* dart poyson out." p. 19.

The Elizabethans were never tired of mentioning the hyena, the crocodile, the chameleon, Proteus, the basilisk etc.: just as these were mere fictions in their imaginations, so Machiavelli had become a kind of allegorical personification of all villainy; the counterpart of the devil. Thus in "Friar Bacon's Prophecie: A Satire on the Degeneracy of the Times", the brazen head introduced to the Elizabethan audience by Greene says: —

"How observation findes
By all experience artes,
How Machavilian mindes
Do plaie the devils partes;
While love, (alas!) hath little grace
In worshipping a wicked face."
Percy Soc. (Halliwell) XV. p. 15.

The same use is made in denouncing Sir Walter Raleigh as a Machiavellian.

---

[1]) Cf. "From female Machiavell pull thou the maske
— — — — from daughter to the Devill" **23**. *ibid.*

"Wilye Watt, wilie Wat,
Wots thou not and know thou what,
Looke to thy forme and quat
    In towne and citie.

Freshe houndes are on thy taile,
That will pull downe thy saile,
And make thy hart and quaile
    Lord for the pittie.

—   —   —   —

For thy skaunce and pride,
Thy bloudy minde beside,
And thy mouth gaping wide
    Mischievous Machiavell.

Essex for vengeance cries,
His bloud upon the lies,
Mounting above the skies
    Damnable fiend of hell,
    Mischevous Matchivell."
Percy Soc. No. 55, VII.

Robert Pricket defended Essex from the very crime just imputed to his rival.

„He [Essex] was not hollow, like the Vaults of hell,
His soundnesse fled from base hypochrisy.
He fetcht no rules from hel-borne Machiavel, [1]
  His learning was divine Philosophy,
His word and deed without a false intending,
In Honors Lyft went on, the Truth commending;
  His vertues steps to Truth inclinde,
  Close subtile falshood underminde."
Honors Fame. Grosart. 33.

Breton continued in his cant use. [2]

---

[1] Cf. Cowper "Charity" (Chalm. XVIII, 635).
"Where love, in these the World's last doting years,
As frequent as the want of it appears

—   —   —   —

The statesman, skill'd in projects dark and deep,
Might burn his useless Machiavel, and sleep."

[2] Grimello) "I loved no Painting on my face ... nor excesse in

In Shakspere's "Othello" Jago is a thorough Italian villain: his playing off of Roderigo and Cassio is not "un — Machavilian", but still shows no direct knowledge of the "Principe". The only thought, which might possibly come from this book, is of frequent occurence in Shakspere.

"Dull not device by coldness and delay." II, 3.

In Marston and Webster's "Malcontent" Mendoza is a "villainous politician", but rather a shallow one. His scheme, of using Malevole to kill the duke, and then to kill him, is that so often found already in the drama; he has, however, all the egoism of a Machiavel.

"We that are great, our sole self-good still moves us."
IV, 1 (Bullen I, 283).

He cites two Machiavellian maxims, both of which had appeared before in English literature.

"They [Piero and Malevole] shall die both, for their deserts
Than we can recompense."[1]) IV, 1 (291).   [crave more

"Mischief that prospers, men do virtue call.[2])
I'll trust no man: he that by tricks gets wreaths
Keeps them with steel." V, 2 (306).

These show, as before stated, that Marston had studied the "Prince". The very blunder through which Mendoza fails Machiavelli had warned against. [3])

---

my apparrell ... nor to flatter a foole, nor to converse with a Macha-vilion, make idle love" — Grimello's Fortune: Grosart. II, 6.

[1]) Vide "Leicester's Commonwealth" — Buckingham and Rich. III. p. 23.

[2]) Cf. Behn: "The Feign'd Curtezans" V, 2 (II, 329).
Cornelia) — "for Wisdom is but good Success in things, and those that fail are Fools.
Galliard) Most gloriously disputed!
You're grown a Machivellian in your Art."

[3]) Mend.) "The chiefest secret for a man of state
Is, to live senseless of a strengthless hate." V, 2 (307).

(1605)

In Sylvester's "Du Bartas" of this year, England is accused of using Machiavellian principles.

— "the Translator (leaving his translation) sharply citeth England

> And wanton *England*, why hast thou forgot
> Thy visitation, as thou had'st it not
>
> — — — —
>
> Thine uncontroll'd, bold, open *Atheism*
> Close *Idol-service:* cloaked Hypocrism
>
> — — — —
>
> Strife-full *Ambition, Florentizing* States
> *Bribes and Affection* swaying Magistrates
>
> — — — —
>
> These are thy sins: These are the *Signes* of Ruin."
>
> 2nd day of 1st week.

In the comedy of the "London Prodigal", once attributed to Shakspere, occurs the following:

> Master Flowerdale) "Good morrow, good Sir Lancelot: good morrow, master Weathercock. By my troth, gentlemen, I have been reading over Nick Machiavel, I find him good to be known, not to be followed. A pestilent human fellow! I have made certain annotations on him, such as they be."
> III, 2 (Anc. Brit. Dram. 383.)

This idea of annotations is, of course, a reminiscence of Greene, who probably had his notion from Nashe. When Sir Lancelot presses Flowerdale to tell him if he have a duel on hand with Oliver, he rejoins: —

> "The Italian hath a pretty saying. Questo — I have forgot it too: 'tis out of my head: but in my translation, if it hold, thus: If thou hast a friend, keep him; if a foe, trip him."
> III, 2.

Machiavelli expressly says that hate is fatal. Prin. XVII. So Hanno in "Sophonisba": —

> "'Tis well in state
> To doe close ill, but voyd a public hate." II, 3 (627).

No such maxim occurs in Machiavelli, and there are none of his supposed teachings in this play; but certainly, it was not unintentional that this wretched profligate was made to read Machiavelli: no doubt, the audience saw in such reading the source of all his licentiousness.

Chapman, with his excellent Terencian comedy "All Fooles", now sought to ridicule the popular conception of Machiavellism in Gastanzo, a simple old fool who, however, boasts himself

> — "acquainted
> With the fine sleights and policies of the world." ·
>
> III, 1 (Shepherd 62).

He is duped by everybody, but tenaciously considers all except himself fools. He is the parodied Machiavel.

Valerio, believed by his father Gastanzo too bashful even to speak to a woman, is a very rake: he meets, and embraces his "stolen wife" Gratiana of whom Gastanzo had no knowledge. The wily Rinaldo says: —

> "And should the wretched Machiavelian
> The covetous knight, your father, see this sight,
> Lusty Valerio?" I, 1 (49).

Again, when Rinaldo actually cozens the old simple-ton into taking Gratiana in his own house, as Fortunio's wife:

> Rin.) "And work all this out of a Machiavel, [1])
> A miserable politician
> I think the like was never played before." II, 1 (57).

---

[1]) Cf. Otway: "Friendship in Fashion" V (p. 59 ed. Thorn.).

Mrs. Goodvile (Lettice having reported her husband is coming home disguised to deceive her) "Mr. Truman, do you retire with Malagene. I'll stay here, and receive this Machiavel in disguise."

Gastanzo's Machiavellism consists in the following
evident parody: —

> "Promises are no Fetters: with that tongue
> Thy promise past, unpromise it againe,
> Wherefore has Man a Tongue, of powre to speake
> But to speake still to his owne private purpose?
> Beastes utter but one sound; but Men have change
> Of speach and Reason, even by Nature given them:
> Now to say one thing, and an other now,
> As best may serve their profitable endes."   II, 1 (55).

In "Eastwarde Hoe", Borgia [1]) is cited much in the
manner Machiavelli ordinarily was. In Heywood's play,
"If you know not me", recurs the old thought in "Tancred
and Gismunda":

Winchester to Mary.)   "If your highness
                    Will your own estate preserve, you must
                    Foresee far danger, and cut off all such
                    As would your safety prejudice." Sh. Soc. 197 (1851).

In "Volpone", Jonson introduced a very facetious use
of the popular "scare": —

Sir Politick) First, for your garb, it must be grave and serious,
                    Very reserv'd and lock'd: not tell a secret
                    On any terms — — — — beware
                    You never speak at ruth —
        (Peregrine) How!
    Sir Pol.) Not to strangers — — — —
                    And then, for your religion, profess none,
                    But wonder at the diversity, of all:
                    And, for your part, protest, were there no other
                    But simply the laws o'the land, you could content you,
                    Nic. Machiavel, and Monsier Bodin, both
                    Were of this mind. Then must you learn the use
                    And handling of your glass; (these are main matters

---

[1]) Quick.)   "Bring forth my braverie.
    Now let my truncks shoote forth their silkes conceal'd.
    I now am free, and now will justifie
    My trunkes and punkes. Avaunt, dull flat-cap, then!
    Via, the curtaine that shadowed Borgia!" II, 1.

With your Italian:) and to know the hour
When you must eat your melons, and your figs.
Per.) Is that a point of state too?
Sir Pol.) Here it is." IV, 1 (375).

In this scene, as Whalley observed and Gifford accepted, Jonson ridicules the advice usually given for Italian travel; it is also evident he has adopted Chapman's bantering sarcasm on Machiavelli.

(1606).

In the year 1606 Barnabe Barnes cited Machiavelli thrice in his "Offices": one citation treats of the maxim often found in the drama. Thus in the dedication to King James: —

> "Vile is that wretched analogie, which the corrupt Florentine Secretarie *Nicolo Machivelli* servant to Duke *Petro di Medici*, did in his puddle of princely policies produce betwixt a true Prince and a mixt monster: resembling him (by the example of *Achilles* who was instructed by *Chyron* the Centaure) unto a lion and a fox, importing his strength and caution in all affaires: whereas it is well knowen, how no true prince can aptly be compared to that unsavory curre. ... Il Prencipe cap. 18."

The two other references never occur in the drama; [1] all three are, of course, refuted or denied. [2] Marston again

---

[1] "It is very commendable in a prince to be reputed liberall, which some curious and cunning writers would have out of the purses of others .... Nicolo Macc. il pren. cap. 16." p. 12.

[2] e. g. "There is one ambitious rule, which the Machivilian politicks have taught to colour their wickednesse, according to that saying out of *Euripides* cited by *Cicero* from the mouth of *Caius Caesar*: *Nam si violandum est jus, regnandi gratia violandum est*; *alijs rebus pietatem colas*: For if men will violate justice, the violation thereof ought to proceed from the hopes of soveraignitie, which may depend thereon: in all other things (saving in matters of empire) let a man declare pietie. But the wisest Philosophers teach us, that it is base and vulgar to thirst after soveraignitie; meaning that ambition can not seaze upon

shows in Sophonisba his intimate knowledge of the "Prince".

Syphax) "Passion is reason when it speakes from might:
I tell thee, man, nor kings nor gods exempt,
But they grow pale if once they find contempt."[1])

I, 1 (Bullen II, 242).

so also: —

Carthalo). "Pish! prosperous successe gives blackest actions glorie;
The meanes are unremembered in most story."[2]) II, 1 (255).

again,

Asdrubal has given order for Massinissa's murder: —

Hanno) "But yet thinke, Asdruball,
'Tis fit at least you bear griefe's outward show;
It is your kinsman bleeds. What need men know
Your hand is in his wounds? 'Tis well in state
To doe close ill, but voyd a public hate."[3]) II, 3 (267).

and again: —

Hanno) "Profit and honesty are not in one state" II, 1 (254).

Although this last line savors of Marlowe, yet there can be no doubt, but that three of these passages go directly to the "Principe", as well as the following often found before: —

Carthalo) — "violent chance shall force a state
To break given faith.
Beware t'offend great men, and let them live."[4]) II, 1 (256).

Medice or, as he confesses himself, "Mendice" in the "Gentleman Usher" was a fitting study for Lorenzo in "Al-

---

a very noble and magnanimious heart. . . . Vide cap. 17 prince Nic. Machiavell." p. 110.
[1]) Cf. Prin. XIX: Disc. III, 6 (329).
[2]) Prin. XV. Ante 105, note 2.
[3]) Prin. XVII.
[4]) Ante p. 24.

phonsus", but Machiavellian maxims were not, as yet, used seriously by Chapman.

(1607)

Having made acquaintance with Machiavelli, Barnes now sought to incorporate his knowledge in a play, "The Divel's Charter" [1]), containing the life and death of Alexander VI and Caesar Borgia. The play is a palpable imitation of Marlowe; the Pope signing the blood compact, conjuring and dying as Faustus had done. [2]) It is a mixture of murder, adultery, incest, homicide, fratricide, and sodomy seldom surpassed. No mention is made of Machiavelli, but the "Principe" [3]) is used to considerable extent in the first act. So: —

Alex. to Candy) "You must not be so ceremonius
        Of oathes and honesty, Princes of this world
        Are not prickt in the bookes of conscience,
        You may not breake.your promise for a world:
        Learne this one lesson — looke yee marke it well,
        It is not alwaies needfull to keepe promise,
        For Princes (forc'd by meere necessity
        To passe their faithfull promises) againe
        Forc'd by the same necessity to breake promise."   I, 4.

---

[1]) No doubt, the same as "Alexander VI", entered on the Stationer's registers Oct. 16th, 1607, though Halliwell (Dic. of Plays p. 9) does not notice it as such.

[2]) Guicciardini acts as prologue just as Machiavelli did for the "Jew of Malta".

[3]) Sforza's words to Charles also arise from it:
     "Can more grosse error rest in pollicy,
     Then first to raise a turbulent sharpe storme,
     And unadvisedly to leave defence
     To doubtful chance and possibilities.
     To brooch strong poyson is too dangerous,
     And not be certaine of the present vertue
     Which is contained in his Antidot.
     Wilde fire permitted without limit burnes,
     Even to consume them that first kindled it."
                   I, 1. Cf. Prin. III.

and this: —

> Caesar) "And for your more instructions learne these rules!
> If any Cedar in your forrest spread,
> And overpeere your branches with his top
> Provide an axe to cut him at the roote,
> Suborne informers or by snares intrap
> That King of Flies within the Spider's Webbe;
> Or else ensnare him in the Lion's toyles.
> What though the multitude applaud his fame:
> Because the vulgar have wide open eares,
> Mutter amongst them, and possesse their hearts
> That his designements wrought against the state,
> By which yea wound him with a publicke hate:
> So let him perish yet seeme pittiful.
> Cherrish the weakenesse of his stock and race
> As if alone he meritted disgrace.
> Suffer your Court to mourne his funeralls,
> But burne a bone-fire for him in your Chamber."

to which Alexander adds: —

> "*Caesar* delivereth Oracles of truth.
> 'Tis well-sayd Caesar, yet attend a little,
> And binde them like rich bracelets on thine armes
> Or as a precious iewell at thine eare.
> Suppose two factious Princes both thy friends,
> Ambitious both, and both competitors,
> Advance in hostile armes against each other:
> Joyne with the strongest to confound the weake,
> But let your war's foundation touch his Crowne,
> Your neerest charity concerne yourself;
> Els let him perish: yet seeme charitable,
> As if you were meerely compos'd of vertue:
> Beleeve me, *Candy*, things are as they seeme,
> Not what they be themselves: all is opinion:
> And all this world is but opinion."[1] I. 4.

But even Barnes mixes up Machiavelli and Marlowe, thus:

> "Look what large distance is twixt Heaven and Earth,
> So mony leagues twixt wealth and honesty:

---

[1] Prin. XXI.

> And they that live puling upon the fruits
> Of honest consciences, starve on the Common." I, 4.

This idea of wealth can only come from Barabas: the last two lines, certainly, are taken almost literally from him. [1])

Caesar is a Machiavellian, [2]) and makes use of the stratagem so often met with in the drama. He has Frescobaldi kill Candy, and then kills the assassin by pitching him into the Tiber. Thus we see, a dramatist, using the "Principe" with malice afore-thought, could not keep himself free from the powerful influence of Marlowe.

Beaumont and Fletcher now took it upon themselves also to parody the Machiavel villain of the stage in the person of Lucio (in "The Woman Hater"), a weak formal statesman, ever racking his brains, "For the main good of the dear commonwealth". The formal fool [3]) says of himself: —

> "My book-strings are suitable, and of a reaching colour . . .
> My standish of wood strange and sweet, and my fore-flap
> hangs in the right place, and as near Machiavel's as can be
> gathered from tradition." V, 1. (Darley II, 447.)

The Duke sees through his littleness however: the passage, being characteristic of the reason why in so many

---

[1]) Ante p. 4ϕ.ϕ

[2]) Cf. Lee: "Caesar Borgia" I, 1 (II. 18 ed. 1734).

Machiavel) "O! *Caesar Borgia*! such a Name and Nature!
   That is my second Self; a *Machiavel*!

[3]) For a fool to think himself a Machiavel was also popular after the Restoration.

E. g. Cibber: "The Double Gallant" IV, 1 (III, 63).

Sir Solomon Sad-life (a gulled cuckold). "What two blessed escapes I have had! to find myself no Cuckold at last, and, which had been equally terrible, my Wife not know I wrongfully suspected her. — Well! at length I am fully convinc'd of her Virtue — and now if I can but cut off the abominable Expence, that attends some of her impertinent Acquaintance, I shall show myself a *Machiavel*."

Meyer, Machiavelli.

Italian ¹) plays, where villains abound, so little Machiavellism occurs in Beaumont and Fletcher, is here given: —

Duke) "Why thinks your lordship I am up so soon?
Lucio) About some weighty state-plot.
Duke) You are well conceited of yourselves to think
    I chuse you out to bear me company
    In such affairs and business of state!
    Weightier far:
    You are my friends and you shall have the cause;
    I break my sleeps thus soon to see a wench." ²) I. 1 (429).

In the final dismissal of Lucio, the dramatists must have had in mind Machiavelli's study in his banishment.

Out of Lazarillo's plot to get a taste of the Umbrana's head Lucio has convicted him of High Treason.

Valerio) „Sir, you have performed the part of a most careful statesman; and, let me say it to your face sir, of a father to this state: I would wish you to retire, and insconce yourself in study; for such is your daily labour, and our fear, that your loss of an hour may breed our overthrow." V, 2 (450).

(1608)

In the next year ³) (1608) appeared the second edition of Patericke's translation of Gentillet.

---

¹) "A duke there is, and the scene lies in Italy as though two things lightly, we never miss." Prologue. 428.

²) Machiavelli expressly forbids intriguing with subjects' wives. Prin. XVII: Ist. Fior. II (123): Disc. III, 26 (395). Prin. XIX.

³) This was the year of Lord Brooke's "Alaham". Lamb says in his "Specimens" of this play and „Mustapha": —

"These two tragedies of Lord Brooke might with more propriety have been termed political treatises than plays. Their author has strangely contrived to make passion, character, and interest of the highest order subservient to the expression of State dogmas and mysteries. He is nine parts Machiavel and Tacitus, for one part of Sophocles and Seneca." This statement like all Lamb's wants to be taken *cum grano salis*.

Beaumont and Fletcher's play "Philaster" contains one thought of the "Principe"; but one already extant in the drama.

> King) "To give a stronger testimony of my love
> Than sickly promises (which commonly
> In princes find both birth and burial
> In one breath) we have" — I, 1 (Darley 28).

John Day showed in his drama "Humour out of Breath" what the prevalent idea of Machiavellians was.

Aspero, the malcontent son of the banished duke Anthonio relates his dream, and asks his father to do the same: —

Anth.) "How can he dream that never sleeps, my sonne?
Asp.) O, best of all: why, your whole world doth nothing but dreame: your machiavell he dreames of state, deposing kings, grounding new monarchies: the lover, he dreames of kisses" —

> I, 2 (Bullen 14).

and again:

Asp.) "Send him a letter that I come to kill him.
Boy) Twere great valor, but little pollicy, my Lord.
Asp.) How long have you bin a matchiavilian, boy?
Boy) Ever since I practis'd to play the knave, my lord.
Asp.) Then policy and knavery are somewhat a kin.
Boy) As neere as penury and gentry: a degree and a half remov'de, no more." II, 1.

These passages merely voice what has already been heard; but still there is one significant point about them. All the other names of persons, of which several occur in

---

There is very little Machiavellianism in "Alaham" other than his egoism:

e.g. *Heli*) "Thou art but one: for all a sufferer be.
Alah.) That one is more than all the world to me."

> I, 1 (Grosart III, 473).

But these two plays are "closet-dramas" -and lie beyond the discussion on hand.

this play, are spelt with initial capitals: this one alone, in two places, appears without. The conclusion must be, that it had passed, for the day at least, from a proper into a common noun, just as "braggadoccio" and "gnathonic" have done. [1]) This is the more remarkable, since Machiavelli was an historical personage and not a mere fiction as Braggadoccio and Gnatho. Whether the explanation offered be right or not, this use occurs here alone, and was even discarded by Day himself in another play.

> Horatio) "What is a Man? hart a the Devil, meere fool.
> His rich invention, Machivilian plots —
> Idle, illusive, antick phantasies,
> Apelles grapes!" *Law-Tricks* 1V, 3.

The "scholarly and cultured" Day shows no knowledge of Machiavelli, other than the mere cant name in his individual plays; this makes it doubtful whether it was he or Haughton, who (it was conjectured) adapted Belphegor.

(1609)

In 1609 J[ohn] M[elton] cited Machiavelli's advice as to religion, and punned upon his name.

"Fiftly, let him resolve himselfe

> to be immooveably fixed .... in his religon, ... *Machiavill* therefore (whether men tearme him *Hatchevil*, or not to be macht in evill, it bootes not) in this respect perswades his schollers wisely (in my poore conceit) either not at all to devote himselfe to any religion, or else never to forsake their conscience: either to be absolutely good or absolutely ill, not to hong in uncertaintie, sometimes inclining to good actions, sometimes to ill, as they best seeme to further their present use and imployment." *A Sixe-Folde Politician.* 158.

---

[1]) A similar use of Aretine is made in "A Sixefolde Politician" 1609. "They fall either to the secret profession and practicing ... such aretin" — p. 68.

John Davies referred to the egoism of the Florentine's followers: by making the same *jeu de mot* as the preceeding, he proves the name was pronounced Match-, not Mach-iavel.[1]) Dekker, in a pamphlet "Worke for Armorours", made his only reference to Machiavelli, and adopted the popular idea of all deception having originated with him.

> "Deceipt lookes a little squint, yet is of deeper reach than any of the rest [Violence, Usury, etc.] .... He hath more followers than the 12 Peeres of Fraunce, he studies *Machiavell*, and hath an french face." Grosart IV, 131.

(1610)

In the next year (1610) Davies finished his characteristic citations of Machiavelli, (punning again on the word), by proclaiming him hung up in hell for his devilish precepts, which even all grooms were now practicing.

> "But now (ah now) ensues a pinching pang,
> A villaine vile, that sure in hell doth hang,
> Hight *Mach-evill* that *evill* none can match,
> Daub'd me with dev'llish Precepts, Soules to catch,
> And made me so, (poore silly innocent)
> Of good soules wracke, the cursed instrument.
> Now not a Groome (whose wits erst soard no hyer
> Then how to pile the Logs on his Lords fire)
> But playes the *Machiavillian* (with a pox)
> And in a Sheep-skin clad, the Woolfe or Fox."
>
> *Paper's Complaint.* Grosart II, 78.

Muleasses in John Mason's "The Turke" is an overdrawn imitation of Eleazar. His maxim is: —

> "When Truth's sonnes play the Polititians,
> Heav'n help thee, Truth, in Earth thy case is hard:
> Truth's hardly matcht with Machiavelians,
> That her wil wound so they themselves may ward:
> For, pious Polititians are blacke swans:
> And blest are Realmes that they do (ruling) gard:"
>
> *Humours Heav'n on Earth.* Grosart I, 25.

"murder and blood
Are the two pillars of a Statesman's good." II, 1.

Borgias is also a villain of the deepest dye; but there
is no Machiavellianism in the play.

(1611)

In Dekker's play of 1611, "If't be not Good, the Devill
is in't", one of the devils, sent by Pluto bears the name
of Alphege: whether this be a reminiscence of "Belphegor"
or not, the beginning of this play, as Langbaine [1]) observes,
seems to be written in imitation of the novelette.

Jonson's "Cataline" contains thoughts to be found in
the "Principe"; but what was said of "Sejanus" [2]) applies
here as well: morever both the following thoughts were
already in the drama.

Cic.) — "for unto men
Prest with their wants, all change is ever welcome." [3])
III, 2 (Giff-Cunn. II, 105).

Caes.) (to Cat.) — "and slip no advantage
That may secure you. Let them call it mischief;
When it is past and prospered 'twill be virtue." [4])

(1612)

Sylvester again accuses the court of using Machiavelli: [5])
in "Simile non est idem".

---

[1]) Mom. Trium. ad locum.
[2]) Ante 78. p 100
[3]) Cf. Prin. III: Disc. III, 21 (380).
[4]) This was a direct plagiarism on Ben's part. Cf. Marston "Malcontent" V, 2 (ante p. 81):
"Mischief that prospers men do virtue call."
[5]) Again he uses Florentine for Mach. in "Lacrymae Lacrymarum":
"Let each of us cease to lament (in vain)
Prince Henry's Loss: Death is to *Him* a Gain
For Savoy's Dukelings, or the *Florentine,*
Hee weds his *Saviour* of a Regall *Line.*" II, 278.

"Sacred *Religion* where art thou?
Not in the *Church*, with *Simonie*:
Nor on the *Bench*, with Briberie:
  Nor in the *Court*, with *Machiavell*:
Nor in the *Citie*, with *Deceits*:
Nor in the Country, with Debates
  For What hath *Heav'n* to do with *Hell*?"
          Grosart II, 255.

He condemns it again for so doing: in "Panaretus".

"But to His [God's] onely Bountie must they [Princes] give
Th'honour of all the fruits they shall atchieve
By their most noble Cares, most royall Pains:
Not to the depth of Machiavilian brains." II, 132.

He also has a strange passage, where he links the
two most abhorred Italians together: in "Lacrymae Lacrymarum".

"All, briefly all, all Ages, Sexes, Sorts,

—   —   —

All Epicures, Wit-wantons, Atheists,
Mach-Aretines, Momes, Tap-to-Bacconists

—   —   —

Have pull'd this waight of *Wrath*; the *Vengeance* down."
            II, 278.

Webster, having in mind, no doubt, the Medici to whom
the "Principe" was dedicated, took occasion to call Francisco
de Medici a Machiavellian in his tragedy "The White
Devil".

Fran.) "Sure, this was Florence' doing [the murder of Brachiano].
Flam.) Very likely.
Those are found weighty strokes which come from the hand,
But those are killing strokes which come from the head.
O, the rare tricks of a Machiavelian!
He doth not come, like a gross plodding slave,
And buffet you to death, makes you die laughing,
As if you had swallow'd down a pound of saffron.
You see the feat, 'tis practis'd in a trice;
To teach court honesty, it jumps on ice."
         V, 3 (Mermaid Ser. 104).

In another passage direct reference seems to be made to the "Principe".

Brach. to physician) "Most corrupted politic hangman,
You kill without book." [1])   V, 3 (96).

Francisco uses Machiavellian maxims: Gasparo says to Vittoria of him: —

"Fool, princes give rewards with their own hands,
But death or punishment by the hands of others." V, 6 (121).

This is one of Machiavelli's points of praise in Cesare Borgia. [2])

Brachiano, too, has much of the Florentine in him: Lodowick says to him: —

"Oh you slave!
You that were held the famous politician [3])
Whose art was poison." V, 3 (102).

There is, however, little or no direct Machiavellism in this play; since it contains no political intrigue, but is based on that action in the prince Brachiano, which Machiavelli expressly forbids.[4])   None of Webster's other preserved [5]) plays makes use of the Florentine.

---

[1]) Nashe had already said: — "The art of Murder Machiavel hath penn'd."

[2]) Cf. Prin. VII.

[3]) Romelio says he could play the villain in "The Devil's Law Case",

"As if I had eat a politician,
And digested him to nothing but pure blood."
III, 2 (Dyce. 122).

This probably means Machiavelli.

[4]) Ante p. 87 note 3.

[5]) In the letter to Finch prefixed to "The Devil's Law-Case" Webster speaks of a play "The Guise", by himself; this, through Marlowe's influence, may have contained Machiavellism. Cf. Dyce 105. Tourneur, whose name is often placed unjustly by Webster's, seems to have had no knowledge of Machiavelli.

(1613)

In 1613 appeared a curious poem, "The Uncasing of Machivil's Instructions to his sonne: With the Answere to the same", [1]) which promulgates the time-honored theory, advocated if not invented by Cardinal Pole, that the "Principe" was written only as a warning.

> "Machiavil's rules doe whet the purest wits,
> And doe expell them from their idle fits:
> To wisemen they showe the world's follie,
> With notice of preventing deedes unholie,
> Which is the true intent of the Authors meaning, [showing?]
> How ever fooles their judgements are bestowing.
> Though the beginning doe of harshnesse taste
> And many things are hudléd up in hast:
> And though there be instruction to ill,
> Good understanding the same doth kill,
> And turnes those words unto the truest sense,
> Which for those faults doth make a recompence,
> As the Answere by degrees plainly showes,
> What duty to Vertue each creature owes,
> Condemne not all till all be throughly past,
> If first be worst, the best is kept till last."

The author was evidently exercised at the awful but enticing apparition, which Machiavelli had become to his countrymen, and the prodigal manner in which they were supposed to be practising his precepts. Nevertheless, he falls into the same cant use of him as the pedagogue of all villainy. [2]) He seems to have known no more of the Florentine, than such maxims as were already notorious: —

---

[1]) Cf. Lowndes "Bib. Man." III, 1438.

[2])   "— the poore man, that pines for want of friends:
> May sit and sigh, and picke his finger's ends.

— — — —

> Till that some good Knight or learned gentleman
> That will not be a Machavillian,

— — — —

> May hap to grace him —" (p. 23).

"If thou wilt be a man of much esteeme,
Be not the same what ever so thou seem,
Speak faire to al, be gentle, courteous, kind,
But let the World know nothing of thy mind.

— — — —

Nor trust no friend, for faith begins to faile:

— — — —

The wisest poore man passeth for a gull." p. 5.

"Promise enough, but not performe to much:

— — — —

Frequent the Church make show of great devotion." p. 6.

"Let conscience knock, care not for that at all." p. 11.

"Look to't in time, strike whiles the iron's hot." p. 14.

"Learne to know kingdomes, Nations, and their natures,

— — — —

But in all noates, noate this of all,
How thou mai'st rise, whoever hap to fall." p. 22.

With these popular ideas of Machiavellism are mixed up the most jejune commonplaces: [1]) we also find the Marlowesque idea of Machiavelli instructing how to make money:

"Looke well about, that thou kast time and place,
Least that some Machiavill chance to spie it,
Dicloseth all, to gaine something by it." p. 9.

Or more direct still: —

"But withall be sure to flatter soe,
That to thy purse, some piece of monie goe."[2]) p. 14.

---

[1]) Such as: "Wear not thy shooes to short, nor cloake to long." p. 8.
  "Stumble not at a straw, nor leape o're a block;
  Leave not things at randome, keepe all under lock." p. 16.
  "Foule words corrupt good manners." p. 18.
  "But let thy profit answere thy expense,
  Least want do prove a wofull patience,
  And thou do prove the proverbe often tolde,
  A careless *Courtier* yong, a *Beggar* olde." p. 7.
[2]) Also: "Be rich therefore I say, be rich my *Sonne*,
  For wealth will sway the World when all is done." p. 27.

and this leads to a thought also to be found in one of the dramatic villains: —

"If thou be rich, thou quickly ma'ist be great."[1]) p. 24.

In the "Answere" the author repeats the *double entendre* idea of Machiavelli's writings: —

— "by the knowledge of them thou might'st beware
How thou art caught in any vicious snare.

— — — —

Machiavel's rules deny, yet use them to thy pleasure."[2])

For each vicious maxim of the first part a virtuous *vade mecum* is given, as: —

"Performe thy word, but promise not too much."
"Frequent the church with faith and true devotion."
"Machiavel's rules let Machiavels reade,
Love thou thy God, his spirit be thy speede."

and the stalest proverbs are again rung in.[3])

Machiavelli had now become such a public scare-crow as to appear to the shrewd Henslowe a capital catch-penny: we find him paying over double the sum usually given for a play to Robert Daborne for his tragedy of "Machiavel and The Devil".[4])

„Memorandum: 'tis agreed between Phillip Hinchlow, Esqr and Robert Daborn, gent., y^t ye s^d Robert shall before ye end of this Easter Term deliver in his Tragoedy, cald Matchavill and ye Divill, into the

---

[1]) Cf. Marston "Malcontent".
Mal.) — "make me some rich knave, and I'll make myself some great man." III, 4.

[2]) Again: "But now my sonne, that thou hast learn'd this lore,
Upon my blessing looke on it no more,
Except it be by ill to know the good."

[3]) "Familiarity contempt doth breed."
"A meane in all, in all is ever best."

[4]) Cf. Hazlitt's Man. p. 146.

hands of ye s^d Phillip . . . . This 17th of Aprill 1613."
Alleyn Papers ed. Coll., p. 56;
and farther on: —

"Mem: I have receaved of Mr Hinchlow the full somm of sixteen pounds, in part of twenty pounds due to me, Robert Daborne, for my tragoedy of Matchavill and the Divell . . . . Robt. Daborne.

Collier supposed this might refer to Belphegor. [1]) His conjecture must stand as only of very doubtful value: the play is expressly called in both notices a tragedy: a tragedy could hardly have been written upon Belphegor, so eminently comical. More likely it was some such production as a combination of the Jew of Malta and Faustus, where Machiavelli sold his soul to the devil, as Alexander VI in the "Divel's Charter". It is certainly to be regretted that no copy of this play, in which Machiavelli was for the third time brought on the popular stage, has as yet been found: perhaps it was never printed.

In Chapman's "Revenge of Bussy D'Ambois" Machiavelli is again reverted to, and his maxims, from Gentillet, used. Marlowe called Guise a Machiavellian: Chapman has him use the term with contempt, taking an entirely different view of him than his predecessor did; making him in every way noble. [2])

---

[1]) "It perhaps related to Machiavelli's novel of Belphegor, in which the devil plays so principal a part: . . . . The price of a new play at this date had risen [from 10] to 20 lbs." l. c., p. 56.

[2]) See the grand monologue just before his assassination (p. 209). Even the Massacre is forgiven him (p. 190). Dryden also was more lenient with Guise: in his play it is King Henry who is the Machiavelian: thus "The Duke of Guise". II, 1 (Scott VII, 40):

King).;"O this whole Guise . . . . Might I but view him, after his plots
and plunges
Stuck on those cow'ring shallows that await him, —
This were a Florence masterpiece indeed."
Again, after Guise's murder:
Queen M.) "You have cut out dangerous work, but make it up
With speed and resolution."

Guise) "These are your Machiavellian villains,
Your bastard Teucers that, their mischiefs done,
Run to your shield for shelter : . . .
. . . . woe be to that state
Where treachery guards and ruin makes men great."

The villains referred to are Baligny and Monsieur
(i. e. D'Alençon): no doubt, Chapman remembered to what
a Machiavellian Gentillet had dedicated his book, receiving
ridicule from him in return. The principles cited, are: —

Baligny) "Treachery for kings is truest loyalty;
Nor is to bear the name of treachery,
But grave, deep policy. All acts that seem
Ill in particular respects, are good
As they respect your universal rule." II, 1 (Shep. 187).

Maillard) "But thus forswearing is not perjury;
You are no pólitician; not a fault,
How foul soever, done for private ends,
Is fault in us sworn to the public good:" IV, 1 (199).

These thoughts may be found in Prin. 15 and 18, but
to insist Chapman had them from there would be hyper-
critical: as we have seen, they were already in the drama.

(1614)

R[ichard] C[orbet] in the next year (1614) denounced
the two most popular maxims: to ruin an enemy by slander,[1])
and to palliate villainy in dissimulation.

King) Yes, I'll wear
The fox no longer, but put on the lion." V, 3 (120).

[1]) "Turnus his enemy would faine supplant,
Yet how to doe it iustly, cause doth want.
His Machiavillian pate doth then devise
To overthrow him by mere forgeries;
Then saith he is a traiter to his prince,
And that he can of treason him convince.

— — — —

Thus armde, he brings to passe his damned will,
And like a villain guiltlesse blood doth spill.

"Another's minde by hate distempered is,
Malicing whom in shew he seems to kisse.
'Tis base affection causeth dismall strife.
Despoileth honour, and destroyeth life.
Yet in these dayes 'tis counted pollicie
To use dissimulation: villanie
Masqu'd under friendships title (worst of hate)
Makes a man live secure and fortunate.
These Machiavillions are the men alone
That thrive i'th' world, and gett promotion.
Was ne're soe bad as some of this damnde broode,
This brood of Caines, these dissembling knaves,
These mankinde-haters, bloody minded slaves,
Which all the world with bloody murders fill,
Laughing one those whom they intend to kill."
                    "The Times Whistle" E. E. T. S. 1871. p. 94.

John Tomkis in his comedy of Albumazar bears
facetious testimony to what shrewdness the popular mind
conceived as coming from the Florentine's teachings.
Sulpitia to Lelio her lover, in jest:

"Peace, peace: now y'are so wise, as if ye had eaten
Nothing but brains and marrow of Machiavel:
You tip your speeches with Italian *motti*,
Spanish *refranes*, and English quoth he's."
                    IV, 13 (Dods. XI, 401).

(1615)

In 1615 appeared a second edition of the strange
poem before noticed. [1]) John Stephens satirized the mania,
with which every would-be politician referred to Machiavelli: [2])

But he and's knights o'the post will post to hell,
That thus their soules unto damnation sell."
                    "The Times Whistle" E. E. T. S. 49.

[1]) "The Uncasing of Machiavel's Instructions to his Sonne."

[2]) "*A simple polititian.* Is a purblind Fox, that pretends Machiavell
should be his sire; but he proves a mungrell: he was taken from
schoole before he had learned true Latine: and therefore in triviall
things only, he partakes with craftinesse: because hee lacks true breed-
ing and true bringing up." *Essays and Char.* ed. Halliwell 161.

he also gave a picture of what he supposed to be a real Machiavel, the coloring of which comes all from the popular dramatic heroes.

"*A sicke Machiavell Pollititian.* Is a baked meate for the devill: .... the villainy which makes him fit for the devil's banquet, is close and private: .... and he findes no shifting pollicy to answere his lowd conscience, but only this, *ars deluditur arte*: meaning that it was lawfull for him to cousen the world, which otherwise would have cousened him. Religious I cannot call him: sacer I may call him justly: for hee among the Romans was entitled sacer, who by the people was generally condemned. .... In health he was like the nymph Echo mentioned in Ovid's fables: for hee was alway deeply in love with his owne pollicy .... he and poyson have bene the most assured friends and familiars. The faculties of his soule are much indebted to the devill: for he hath borrowed many darke inventions from his patterne: .... he will not, in sicknes nor in health seeme careless of religion, as if he wanted piety: .... he will not listen to his hearts meaning, when he shadowes hate or piety with appearance .... he excells in three properties: Wit, Sudden execution, and Envy: .... No marvell though he be daunted when hee remembers the next world, though in a staggering beleefe: for by the warrent of potions, gloves, sallets, privy stabbs, and false accusers, he hath sent so many thither befor him, that hee may justly feare they will sue an appeale against him. .... But after death his name growes old with being odious, like that unfortunate Valerian, whose age was long, but taedious and disgraceful."

"Essays and Char." ed. Halliwell 241.

John Taylor commenced his frequent citations of Machiavelli, of whom he knew no more than the name: the

number of times this most popular writer refers to him is
significant of how certain a catch-word the mere name had
become.

> "The Atheist of the Scriptures can dispute,
> That one would deeme him a Religious man:
> The *Temporizer* to the *Time* will sute,
> Although his *Zeale* be a *Machivillian*."
>
> *Taylor's Urania* (Spen. Soc. p. 3).

Now appeared also the play, mentioned by Steevens
"The Valiant Welshman",[1]) Caradoc, "who lived about the
yere of our Lord 70". In this wretched tragedy, palpably
imitated in part from Shakspere and Jonson, occurs this
passage: —

> *Caradoc*) "Turne thee, Usurper, Harpey of this Clime,
> Ambitious villaine, damned homicide:
> *Monmouth*) Fondling, thou speakest in too milde consonants,
> Thy angry words cannot awake my spleene:
>
> — — —
>
> Thy Physicke will not worke: these names thou speak'st,
> Fill up each spongy pore within my flesh,
> With joy intolerable: and thy kind salutes
> Of villany, and ambition, befits
> The royall thoughts of Kings: Reade *Machiavell*:
> *Princes that would aspire, must mocke at hell.*
> *Carad.*) Out, thou incarnate Devill: garde thee, slave:
> Although thou fear'st not hell, Ile dig thy grave.
> *Monm.*) Stay, Prince, take measure of me first.
> *Carad.*) The Devill hath done that long ago." I, 3.

There are no less than three desperate villains intent
upon Caradoc's life: Monmouth, Codigune and Gloster. Of
the first we have heard: the other two are simply unex-
purgated editions.

---

[1]) "The Valiant Welshman, or The True Chronicle History of the
life and valiant deedes of Caradoc the Great, King of Cambria, now
called Wales. Written by R. A. Gent. 1615" [2nd ed. 1663].

After Guinever is given to Caradoc: Codigune, alone, says: —

"Now swels the wombe of my invention,
With some prodigious project, and my brayne
Italianates my barren faculties
To Machivilian blacknesse. Welshman, stand fast;
Or by these holy raptures that inspire
The soule of Polititians with revenge,
Black projects, deepe conceits, quaynt villainies,
— — — —
I'll fall my selfe, or pluck this Welchman down.
— — — — Gloster, I know,
Is Natures master-piece of envious plots,
The Cabinet of all adulterate ill
Envy can hatch: with these I will beginne,
To make black envy Primate of each sin.
Now in the heate of all their revelling,
Hypochrisie, Time's best complexion
Smooth all my rugged thoughts, let them appeare
As Brothell sinnes benighted, darkely cleare.
Lend me thy face, good Janus, let mee looke
Just on Time's fashion, with a double face,
And clad my purpose in a Foxe's case."

All this about "envy, hypochrisy, the Foxe's case" etc. had already been used in the drama *satis superque*. Gloster's Machiavellianism consists also in what has been heard before.

"Discourse not what is done, nor how, nor when.
Onely King's wils are Lawes for other men." III. 1.

Codigune goes through the traditional stage villainy of poisoning the king, having himself crowned, and seeking to ruin his enemy (Caradoc in this case) by slander and underhand murder: he is himself killed by Caradoc, of course.

(1616)

Breton again comes to the front in 1616, accusing Machiavelli of having affected the whole world.

"What Mischiefe walkes among the minds of Men?
Will nothing serve theyr discontented Wills?
Must they needs runne into the Devill's denne?
Are these the Scopes of Machivilian skills?
That all the Worlde, with his Infection fills?
Oh God, what Devill could in ill goe further?
Then Pride, in malice, practice hellish Murther?"

>> *An Invective against Treason.* Grosart I, 3.

Marston, who seems to have had some real respect for Machiavelli, took occasion in his "Jack Drum's Entertainment" to ridicule the political rant of the stage and its supposed indebtedness to the "Father of politicians".

Sir Edward Fortune says of those always asking, "What news at court": —

"O, I could burst
At the conjectures, fears, preventions,
And restless tumbling of our tossed brains!
Ye shall have me an empty cask that's furred
With naught but barmy froth, that never travelled
Beyond the confines of his mistress' lips,
Discourse as confidant of peace with Spain,
As if the genius of quick Machiavel
Usher'd his speech."[1]) Simp. *School of Sh.* II, 136.

In Jonson's play, "The Devil is an Ass", the idea of the devil being outwitted is the same as in Machiavelli's "Belphegor"; but there is no direct borrowing.

In "The Honest Lawyer", a play by S. S., the fox-and-lion maxim is reverted to *en passant.*

Vaster.) "By craft more then by strength, all theeves do rise,
Of many politicke knaves you cannot spie one,
The Foxe will have his prey before the Lion." II, 1.

This comes rather from Machiavelli than Plutarch.

---

[1]) Cf. Aphra Behn: "The Emperor of the Moon."

>> I, 1 (vol. IV, 195).

Elaria) "And so religiously believes there is a World there [in the moon] that he [Dr. Baliardo] Discourses as gravely of the People, the Government, Institutions, Laws, Manners, Religion, and Constitution, as if he had been bred a *Machiavel* there."

(1617)

In the next year (1617) appeared another poem using the scare-crow name as a catch-penny title. "Machiavell's Dogge" resembles much the work before mentioned, "The Uncasing of Machavel's Instructions", and, if not by the same author, is certainly an open imitation of his poem even to verbal coincidence. [1]) It is a general satire, contains no supposed maxims, and only refers to the Florentine once to make a double pun upon his name.

> "Doest thou not see, except thou wilt be blinde,
>   How life hath lost the notes of nature's love:
> And wisdome's wordes are helde but as a wind,
>   Where Machavilians matchless villaines prove,
> And Tigres, Foxes, Wolves, Owles, and Apes,
> Beganne the world in shewes of humane shapes." Stanza 2.

(1618)

In Beaumont and Fletcher's "The Loyal Subject", Boroskie is called in the Dram. Pers. "a malicious seducing Counsellor to the Duke"; he well upholds this character in his vile persecutions of the noble Archas. His plan, by which he has the duke entrap and seek to murder him at the banquet (III, 5), as Archas calls it: —

> "The Judas way, to kiss me, bid me welcome,
> And cut my throat,"

is the same Machiavelli makes mention of as employed by Oliverotto da Fermo. [2]) Boroskie plays, however, a very insignificant part and does very little counselling.

---

[1])   "Uncasing":
   "And thou do prove the proverbe often tolde,
   A carelesse *Courtier* yong, a Beggar olde." p. 7.

      „Mach.'s Dogge":
   "No, thinke upon the Proverbe often tolde,
   A carelesse Courtier young, a begger olde." Stanza 35.

[2]) Cf. Prin. VIII.

— 132 —

(1619)

In the next year (1619) Purchas used "Machiavelian spirits" as synonymous with incarnate fiends.

"And even still whence doe our Labyrinthian Braines, Machiavellian Spirits, Incarnate Fiends, learne their SerpentineWindings, Hookes, Crookes, *Protean* Metamorphoses, malicious Subtilties, superfine Plots, Tricks, Quicks, but from abused Learning?[1]) Thus is *Nature* abused to Atheisme." *Microcos.* 583.

Beaumont and Fletcher's play, "The False One", gave birth to an arch-villain, Photinus; his counsels are Machiavellian, but may have come from Plutarch and the drama. He is one who believes that: —

"What in a man sequester'd from the world,
Or in a private person, is preferred,
No policy allows of in a king:
To be or just or thankful, makes kings guilty."

This is the invariable policy of a Beaumont and Fletcher counsellor; they always upheld the divine right of kings. Then follows what certainly comes from Marlowe.

"The stars are not more distant from the earth
Than profit is from honesty:[2]) all the power
Prerogative, and greatness of a prince
Is lost, if he descend but once to steer
His course, as what's right guides him:[3]) Let him leave
The sceptre, that strives only to be good,
Since kingdoms are maintained by force and blood."

I, 1 (Darley 391).

---

[1]) Cf. Nashe, *ante* p. 56.

[2]) Cf. *Phot.*) — "Bold ambition
To dare, and power to do, gave the first difference
Between the king and subject." V, 2 (407).
These ideas are from the prologue to the "Jew of Malta".

[3]) This thought was expressed almost in the same words by Gentillet (III, 27). B. and F. must certainly have had him before them.

Further on is a thought to be found in "Leicester's Commonwealth", and also in the previous drama.

Sept.)　　　"Services done
For such as only study their own ends,
Too great to be rewarded, are returned
With deadly hate: I learned this principle
In his [Photinus'] own school." V, 3 (408).

(1620)

In the "Virgin Martyr" of this year (1620), Diocletian mentions a maxim to be found in the "Principe"; but Massinger may have had in mind the lines from Virgil, which Machiavelli refers to.

"In all growing empires,
Even cruelty is useful: some must suffer
And be set up examples to strike terror
In others, though far off." [1]) I, 1 (Dyce 3).

(1621)

In the next year (1621) appeared Burton's "Anatomy of Melancholy": in it Machiavelli is reverted to no less than fifteen times; [2]) usually, with perfect justness, but at times, even this learned writer fell into the cant use. Thus, for example: —

"Many politicians, I dare not deny, maintain Religion
as a true means, and sincerely speak of it without
hypochrisy, are truely zealous and religious themselves. Justice and Religion are the two chief props
and supporters of a well-governed common-wealth:

---

[1]) Cf. Prin. XVII: "E intra tutti i principi, al principe nuovo è impossibile fuggire il nome di crudele, per essere gli Stati nuovi pieni di pericoli. Onde Virgilio per la bocca di Didone escusa l'inumanità del suo regno per essere quello nuovo, dicendo:

*Res dura, et regni novitas me talia cogunt
Moliri, et late fines custode tueri.*"

[2]) Vide A. of. M. ed. Shilleto-Bullen I, 100, 132, 217, 357: II, 140, 159, 162. 163: III, 120, 314, 378, 385, 425, 439, 445.

but most of them are but *Machiavellians*, counterfeits only for political ends." III, 378 (Shilleto-Bullen).

(1622)

Taylor again cited Machiavelli, adopting the money-idea of Marlowe.

> "If thou hast *money* thou canst want no wit.
> Art thou a damned Matchivillian,
> Thy *money* makes thee held an honest man."
> *Travels of Twelvepence.* Spenser Soc. p. 73.

According to Elze, this was the year of "Alphonsus Emperor of Germany". This is the play in which Chapman makes most use of Machiavellian principles, although the Florentine statesman is not mentioned by name. Lorenzo, the unscrupulous counsellor of Alphonsus, gives him several maxims. [1]) It must now be borne in mind that no Elizabethan dramatist was so thoroughly conservant with French writings as Chapman was. The neglect of this consideration led Ulrici to declare Lorenzo's maxims taken "fast wörtlich aus dem Principe"; [2]) and so it appears *prima facie:* but on closer observation it is perfectly evident, that the same are not taken "fast wörtlich" from the Principe but g a n z w ö r t l i c h from Gentillet. One test will be sufficient. Lorenzo's first maxim runs thus: —

---

[1]) Elze says: "The political state of the Interregnum of the 13th Century, as described by the poet, bore a close resemblance to the anarchy of the Thirty Years' War. The policy of Ferdinand II was based on principles no less Macchiavellistic than those of Chapman's Alphonsus." Ed. Elze 34.

[2]) "Es [Alphonsus] charakterisiert sich hinlänglich gleich durch die erste Scene, in der Alphonsus sich von seinem gelehrten Secretair die fast wörtlich aus dem *Principe* entlehnten Grundsätze Machiavellistischer Staatskunst auseinandersetzen läfst und sie wie ein Schüler sich aufschreibt, aber unmittelbar darauf nicht nur den Zettel zerreisst, sondern den Lehrer vergiftet, damit Niemand existire, der um seine Pläne und Absichten wisse, — obwohl er sie dem Secretair noch gar nicht enthüllt hatte!" Shak. Dram. Kunst. I, 320.

"1. A prince must be of the nature of the lion and
the fox, but not the one without the other." I, 1
(Shepherd 382). [1])

Machiavelli says:

"Essendo adunque un principe necessitato sapere
bene usare la bestia, debbe di quella pigliare la
volpe ed il leone; perchè il leone non si difende dai
lacci, la volpe non si difende da' lupi. Bisogna
adunque essere volpe a conoscere i lacci, e lione a
sbigottire i lupi. Coloro che stanno semplicemente
in sul lione non se ne intendono." XVIII.

Gentillet says:

"Le Prince doit ensuyure la nature du Lyon, et du
Renard: non l'un sans l'autre." 384.

Patericke translates:

"A prince ought to follow the nature of the Lyon
and of the Fox, yet not of the one without the other."

Certainly no more proof is necessary. Chapman drew
from Gentillet. The other five maxims are as follows:

"2. A prince above all things must seem devout; but
there's nothing so dangerous to his state, as to regard
his promise and his oath." [2])

"3. Trust not a reconciled friend, for good turns
cannot blot out old grudges." [3])

---

[1]) Alphonsus answers:
    "The fox is subtle, but he wanteth force;
    The lion strong, but scorneth policy.
    I'll imitate Lysander in this point,
    And where the lion's hide is thin and scant,
    I'll firmly patch it with the foxes fell."
Thus Machiavelli's famous maxim immediately called to mind in
Chapman, Plutarch, which Greene had also used.

[2]) Cf. Gentillet II, 1 and III, 21. Also Prin. 18: Discorsi III, 42.

[3]) Cf. Gent. III, 6. Also Prin. 7: Discorsi III, 4: Ist. Fior. IV
(217). Lee puts it thus in "Caesar Borgia": —
  Mach.) "None ought to offend his Prince, and after trust him."
                             II, 1 (op. cit. 27).

"4. 'Tis more safety for a prince to be feared than loved." [1])

"5. To keep an usurped crown, a prince must swear, forswear, poison, murder, and commit all kinds of villainies, provided it be cunningly kept from the eye of the world. [2])

In this "poison, murder, and all kinds of villainies", the influence of Marlowe and the drama is plainly visible.

"6. Be always jealous of him that knows your secrets. [3])
And therefore it behoves you credit few,
And when you grow into the least suspect,
With silent cunning must you cut them off."

This last is not to be found exactly as stated either in Machiavelli or Gentillet, but must have been perverted by the dramatists from Principe 23. We have had this, as all other of these maxims, in the drama before Chapman. [4]) It is almost needless to say, Alphonsus follows all these

---

[1]) Cf. Gent. III, 9. Also Prin. 17: Disc. III, 21: Ist. Fior. II (130). After this Alphonsus says: —
"Love is an humour pleaseth him that loves;
Let me be hated, so I please myself.
Love is an humour mild and changeable,
But fear engraves a reverence in the heart."
Gentillet says: —
Les hommes (dit nostre Florentin) aiment comme il leur plait, et craignent comme il plait au Prince." Op. cit. 375.
Machiavelli says:
"Concludo adunque, tornando all' esser temuto et amato, che amando gli uomini a posta loro, et temendo a posta del principe, deve un principe savio fondarsi in su quello che è suo, non in su quello che è d'altri."
It is perfectly evident Chapman had Gentillet and not Machiavelli before him.
[2]) Cf. Gent. III, 18: also Prin. 18: Disc. II, 13: Ist. Fior. 3 (147).
[3]) Cf. Gent. I, 2. Also Prin. 23.
[4]) After Lorenzo dictates these maxims, Alphonsus kills him with his own poison just as Mendoza attempted to do to Malevole in Marston's "Malcontent".

maxims: he uses force and craft; he never keeps faith; he is always suspicious of the Palatine and Saxony, having wronged them; he swears, forswears, poisons, murders etc., and he immediately kills Lorenzo because he knows his master's secrets. To analyse this well-known play [1]) is beyond the scope of the present essay: suffice it to state, that, following these six principles, Alphonsus gives birth to one of the most monstrous abortions of crime the human mind ever conceived.

Once more in Chapman a reminiscence of Machiavelli-Gentillet is to be found: in "Chabot, Admiral of France": —

Chan.) "Seeming has better fortune to attend it,
　　Than being sound at heart and virtuous." [2])　IV, 1 (539).

This is the only place, however, where the crafty chancellor shows any Machiavellianism. In Beaumont and Fletcher's "The Prophetess" of this year there is a thought, taken directly from the Principe.

Aurelia to Maximinian, who has been made Co-Emperor by Diocletian and is ambitious to gain entire control from Charinus, Diocletian having retired: —

"Hath not your uncle Dioclesian taken
His last farewell o' the world? What then can shake you?"

Max) "The thought I may be shaken, and assurance
That what we do possess is not our own,
But has depending on anothers favour:
For nothing's more uncertain, my Aurelia,
Than power that stands not on his proper basis,
But borrows his foundation." [3])　V, 1 (Darley 19).

---

[1]) Elze thought Pater Larmormain the prototype of Lorenzo (Alphon. 34), but as Ward says, "the likeness ... is little more than what might be traced in half the Macchiavellian counsellors who were a standing figure of the Elizabethan stage." Cf. Ward II, 19.

[2]) Cf. Prin. 18.

[3]) Cf. Prin. 7 and 14.

In another play, "The Beggar's Bush", the cant Machiavellianism of the drama is used, and Plutarch-Machiavelli cited. Hempskirke is the villain of the play, who has set up "Wolfort, usurper of the Earldom of Flanders", as Hubert says: —

> "Raised to it by cunning, circumvention, force,
> Blood, and proscriptions." I, 2 (Darley 209).

To accomplish this he —

> "Killed all that made resistance, cut in pieces
> Such as were servants, or thought friends to Gerard
> Vowing the like to him." III, 1 (218).

Hempskirke, after laying a treacherous plot to have Goswin (Florez) killed, who had wounded him, says: —

> "Thus wise men
> Repair the hurts they take by a disgrace,
> And piece the lion's skin with the fox's case."

(1623)

In Massinger's "The Duke of Milan", probably of the year 1623, one of the Machiavellian maxims is mentioned as an "old saw", — so familiar had it become.

> *Fran.*)   — "and, in spite
> Of the old saw, that says, it is not safe
> On any terms to trust a man that's wronged,
> I dare thee to be false." IV, 1 (Mermaid 67).

In the same play occurs another thought to be found in the Principe, but it might also have been dubbed an "old saw" in the drama.

> "Dangers, that we see
> To threaten ruin, are with ease prevented:
> But those strike deadly, that come unexpected." I, 1 (7).

On the strength of these two passages, the one before given from "The Virgin Martyr", and another to be found in "A New Way to Pay Old Debts", it is to be presumed Massinger was acquainted with Machiavelli, though he never mentions him.

(1624)

Taylor in the next year (1624) again used the popular catch-word.

> "Nor is it a Shepheard's trade, by night or day
> To swear themselves in debt, and never pay.
> Hee's no state-plotting *Machivilian*
> Or Project-monger Monopolitan."
>
> *Taylors Pastoral.* (Spen. Soc. 261.)

In this year appeared Middleton's strange play, "A Game at Chess". Probably the most unpopular man in all England towards the close of James' I reign was poor Gondomar. The Spanish Ambassador was looked upon as the very incarnation of hypocrisy and deceit: if we were to think of what men would be dubbed "Machiavels" by popular opinion at this time, Gondomar would certainly be the first one thought of. Such was the case:

White Kt. shoving *Black Kt.* (Gondomar) into the bag:)
> "Room for the mightiest Machiavel-politician
> That e'er the devil hatch'd of a nun's egg."
>
> V, 3 (Bullen IV, 134).

And he confesses himself as such:

B. Kt.) "My Pawn! — How now, the news?
Pawn.) Expect none very pleasing
> That comes, sir, of my bringing: I'm for sad things.
B. Kt.) Thy conscience is so tender-hoof'd of late,
> Every nail pricks it.
Pawn.) This may prick yours too,
> If there be any quick flesh in a yard on't.
B. Kt.) Mine?
> Mischief must find a deep nail, and a driver
> Beyond the strength of any Machiavel
> The politic kingdoms fatten, to reach mine.
> Prithee, compunction needle-prick'd a little
> Unbind this sore wound.

Pawn.) Sir, your plot's discover'd.
B. Kt.) Which of the twenty thousand and nine hundred
   Four score and five? Canst tell!" III, 1 (65).

His villainy consists as he himself says, in having —

> — "betrayed the White House to the Black,
> Beggar'd a kingdom by dissimulation,
> Unjointed the fair frame of peace and traffic,
> Poison'd allegiance, set faith back" — IV, 2 (95).

One point of this play was imitated from Marlowe: Middleton, not inappropriately, brought Loyola onto the stage to give the induction to the "Game at Chess", just as the elder dramatist did Machiavelli to prologue his "Jew of Malta".

Middleton was familiar with Machiavelli's writings: with the "Istoria Fiorentina" at least. [1]) In another play occurs the same citation of Plutarch's Lysander, so often confounded with Principe 18.

Mrs. Knavesby.) "Best soldiers use policy: the lion's skin
> Becomes the body not when 'tis too great,
> But then the fox's may sit close and neat."
> "Anything for a Quiet Life" III, 1 (Bullen V, 291).

(1625)

Fletcher and Rowley's play of the year 1625, "The Bloody Brother", shows a knowledge of Machiavelli's works. Latorch is "Rollo's Earwig": Rollo tells him to make away with his brother Otto.

> "Make him appear first dangerous, then odious;
> And after, under pretence of safety

---

[1]) The plot of "The Witch" is taken from the same through Belleforest, but so changed as to be more adaptable for the stage, the Queen retaining her purity and the King his life. "Almachildis" is the only name directly borrowed.

Davenant (1629) and William Phillips (1698) both drew from this history. See Hazl. Manual 6 and 193.

For the sick state, the land's and people's quiet,
Cut off his head." [1)] I, 1 (Darley 519).

This is the method, which Machiavelli recommends in
Caesar Borgia's practice. Latorch says to Aubrey: —

"Your counsels coulor not with reason of state,
Where all that's necessary still is just.
The actions of the prince, while they succeed,
Should be made good and glorified, not questioned." [2)]

IV, 1 (530).

Aubrey denounces him as one, —

"That creepst within thy master's ear, and whisperst
'Tis better for him to be feared than loved;
Biddst him trust no man's friendship, spare no blood
That may secure him: 'tis no cruelty
That hath a specious end: for sovereignty
Break all the laws of kind: if it succeed
An honest, noble, and praiseworthy deed." IV, 1 (531).

This is merely the stereotyped Machiavellianism of the
drama. Latorch is a murderer, poisoner, hypocrite, — all
that is apposite to an unconscionable villain. [3)]

Aubrey, standing amidst the corpses at the end, cries
out to Latorch, as if Fletcher himself was thundering his
condemnation upon Machiavelli: —

"Behold the justice of thy practice, villain;
The mass of murders thou hast drawn upon us;
Behold thy doctrine!" V, 2 (539).

In another play by Fletcher about this time, "The Chan-
ces", we find: —

Don J.)   "Dost thou think
The devil such an ass as people make him?
Such a poor coxcomb? such a penny foot-post?

[1)] Ante 24 note 2.
[2)] Cf. Prin. 18.
[3)] He has one trait of Ateukin: he pretends to use astrology.

> Compelled with cross and pile to run of errands?
> With Asteroth, and Behemoth, and Belphagor?"

This probably refers to Dekker's play "Belphegor",
founded on Machiavelli's novelette; just as, "the devil an
ass", is a reminiscence of Jonson.

(1626)

The drama for the next five years seems utterly to
disregard Machiavelli, and even popular literature bocomes
almost taciturn on the subject: the incessant citation had
naturally a palling effect. Breton now closed his long list
of references by reverting again to the wealth idea,[1] introduced by Marlowe, and took leave of the Florentine in
hell as the devil's boon companion and counterpart.

> "Winter: Cards and Dice now begin their harvest,
> and good Ale and sack are the cause of civill warres:
> Machiavel[2] and the Devill are in counsell for de-
> struction, and the wicked of the world make hast to
> hell." "Fantasticks." Grosart II, 7.

He may have had in mind Daborne's lost play "Matchevil and the Devil".

(1628)

John Earle in his "Micro-Cosmographie" (1628) ridiculed
the would-be politicians, who were always referring to
Machiavelli,[3] and gave a picture drawn with some power

---

[1]   "Who doth not see what villanies are wrought,
To gather wealth, the ground of wickednesse:
How many scholers Machavell hath taught,
To fill the earth with all ungodlinesse:
While Witte doth onely worke for wealthinesse.
Who lives in ebbs, and may let in the floods,
But will betray his father for his goods?"
"Pasquile's Mad-Cappe." Grosart I, 8.

[2] Grosart remarks: "*Machiavel*: long a synonym for (almost) Satan
himself." Ibid. p. 16.

[3] "*A too idly reserv'd Man* — Is one that is a foole with discretion:
or a strange piece of Politician, that manages the state of himselfe. His

of what he considered a real "Machiavel", in whose traits
Barabas and Richard III are plainly visible.

"The Worlds wise Man — Is an able and sufficient
wicked man, it is a proofe of his sufficiency that
hee is not called wicked, but wise. A man wholy
determin'd in himselfe and his owne ends, and his
instrument:: herein anything that will doe it. His
friends are a part of his engines, and as they serve
his worke, us'd or laid by. In deed hee knows not
this thing of friend, but if hee give you the name,
it is a signe he ha's a plot on you. Never more active in his businesses, then when they are mixt with
some harm to others: and 'tis best play in this Game
to strike off and lie in place. Successfull commonly
in these undertakings, because hee passeth smoothly
those rubs which others stumble at, as Conscience
and the like: and gratulates himself much in this
advantage: Oathes and falsehoods he counts the
neerest way, and loves not by any meanes to goe
about. Hee has many fine quips at this folly of plaine
dealing, but his tush is greatest at Religion, yet hee
uses this too, and Vertue, and good Words, but is
less dangerously a Devil than a Saint. Hee ascribes
all Honestie to an unpractis'dnesse in the World: and
Conscience to a thing merely for Children. Hee scorns
all that are so silly to trust him, and onely not scornes
his enemie: especially if as bad as himselfe: He feares
him as a man well arm'd, and provided, but sets boldly
on good natures, as the most vanquishable. One that

Actions are his Privie Counsell, wherein no man must partake beside.
He speakes under rule and prescription, and dare not shew his teeth
without *Machiavell.* He converses with his neigbours as hee woulde
in Spaine, and feares an inquisitive man as much as the Inquisition....
Hee ha's beene long a riddle himselfe, but at last finds Oedipusses: for
his over-acted dissimulation discovers him, and men doe with him as
they would with Hebrew letter, spell him backwards, and read him."
Arber, E. R. No. 12, p. 34.

seriously admires those worst Princes as *Sforza*, *Borgia*, and *Richard* the Third: and calls matters of deepe villainy things of difficultie. To whom murders are but resolute Acts, and Treason a businesse of great consequence. One whom two or three Countries make up to this compleatnesse, and he ha's travel'd for the purpose. ʻHis deepest indearment is a communication of mischiefe, and then onely you have him fast. His conclusion is commonly one of these two, either a great Man, or hang'd." Arber p. 60.

(1630)

Grosart says in his introduction to Sir J. Eliot, "The evil designes of men who had poisoned the ears of princes with a jealousy of parliaments, are exposed; and some of the doctrines of Machiavel are held up to scorn."[1]) Eliot recurs to two maxims, both of which have already appeared;[2]) he also cites "Patter contra Machiavel".[3])

Sir Robert Naunton, Master of the court of Wards took occasion in his "Fragmenta Regalia" to call attention

---

[1]) Eliot ed. Grosart I, 155.

[2]) "They [ambitious senators] infuse that jealousy into Princes, as the danger of unsecresie, feare of circumvention, trouble of divisions with their consequents, and the like, taken from Machavell and others of that Leven." "Monarchie of Man" Gros. II, 75.

"Subjects should be kept in affection to their Soveraignes; to which end our lawes laie all faults and errors in the ministers, that noe displeasure may reflect upon the K. and soe Seneca does intimat, *regem debere solum prodesse nocere non sine pluribus*, and Machiavell that great master in his art, who was most indulgent unto princes, and sought to advance all tyrannie, yet in this directs that they should disperse curtesies onlie by themselves and leave injuries and punishments to others, which was also insinuated by the Antients in their fictions of Jupiter giving his thunders from the heavens whom they make *fulmen suum placabile solum mittere pernitiosum aliis tradere.* that which was pleasant was his owne, that which was distastfull came by others." "Apol. for Soc." Gros. II, 123.

[3]) "Patter contra Macciav. *si tu le veux, tu le peux*, as the Frenchman has it in his writing against *Machiavell.*"
Mon. of Man. Gros. II, 61.

to the fact, that Leicester had been read in Machiavelli,
which Father Parsons had long before proclaimed.

"To take him in the observations of his Letters and
Writings (which should best set him off) for such
as fell into my hands, I never yet saw a style or
phrase more seeming religious, and fuller of the streams
of devotion: and were they not sincere, I doubt much
of his well-being; and I may fear he was too well
seen in the Aphorismes and principles of *Nicholas* the
Florentine, and in the reaches of Caesar Borgia."
Arber, E. R. No. 20. p. 29.

In Dekker's "Honest Whore" part 2, the author seems
to have had his own "Belphegor" in mind when giving
Orlando these words: —

"I had rather hang in a woman's company, than in
a man's; because if we should go to hell together,
I should scarce be letten in, for all the devils are
afraid to have any women come amongst them."
V, 2 (Merm. 274).

(1631)

In a book of the next year (1631) called "The Whim-
zies", by Richard Braithwaite (?) Machiavel's writings and
maxims are spoken of as very ambiguous:

"The Jayler — Now some againe will object that he
is a subtile Macchiavel, and loves to walke in the
cloudes, because hee never resolves those with whom
hee deales, but fils them full of doubts, and in the
end ever leaves them in suspence." Ed. Halliwell p. 50.

After all that had been brought forward as Machiavelli's teachings, and the generally confused ideas regarding
him and his supposed followers, this remark seems very
apposite.

In Shirley's play "The Traitor" one of the characters
is called Lorenzo de' Medici: the author seems to have
Machiavelli once in mind. One thought, at least, is to be
found in the Principe:

Lorenzo). " 'Tis policy in princes to create
  A favourite, who must bear all the guilt
  Of things ill managed in the state: if any
  Design be happy, 'tis the prince's own."
                                II, 1 (Giff.-Dyce II, 114).

But this may have been only a dramatic reminiscence [1])
in the last of the Elizabethans, as another passage
certainly was:

Lorenzo) "Some Politician,
  That is not wise but by a precedent,
  Would think me weak for using such an instrument
  As this Depazzi: but I know by proof,
  Such men whom fear and honour make our creatures,
  Do prove safe engines: fools will still obey
  When cunning knaves our confidence betray." [2]) IV, 1 (155).

(1632)

In 1632 Taylor gave the Belphegor legend [3]) a most
remarkable turn; having the devil outwit the women instead

---

[1]) Shirley also continues the stage tradition of associating his
villain with the devil.
Sciar. to Lor.)   — "the devil does
              Acknowledge thee on earth the greater mischief,
              And has a fear, when thou art dead, he shall not
              Be safe in hell."   II, 1 (150).
[2]) Cf. Marston: ante 74.
[3]) "Onely at *Mims*, a Cockney boasting bragger
     In mirth, did aske the women for *Belfwagger*.
     But strait the females like the *Furies fell,*
     Did curse, scold, raile, cast dirt, and stones pell mell,
     But we betook us nimbly to our spurs
     And left them calling us rogues, Knaves, and curs,
     With other pretty names, which I discern'd
     They from their old fore-mothers well had learn'd.
     The reason why they are with rage inflam'd,
     When as they heare *Belfwagger* nam'd,
     Is (as report doth say) there dwelt a Squire,
     Who was so full of love, (or lust's desire)
     That with his faire tongue, Hippocritick-hood,
     By slanderous people 'twas misunderstood)

of being driven into despair by one. It has been impossible
to find any authority for the Waterpoet's version; perhaps
it was his own concoction.

In his "Magnetic Lady" Jonson again sneered at, and
undertook to ridicule the Machiavellian counsellor so long
the demon of the stage. In the Dramatis Personae Bias
is called "a vi-politic, or sub-secretary". Compass says of
him: —

> "A vi-politic
> Or a sub-aiding instrument of state" I, 1 (Gifford II, 401).

and Sir Moth introduces him to Lady Loadstone thus: —

> "I have brought you here the very man, the jewel
> Of all the court, close Master Bias, sister!
> Apply him to your side: or you may wear him
> Here on your breast, or hang him in your ear,
> He's a fit pendant for a lady's tip!
> A chrysolite, a gem, the very agate
> Of state and policy, cut from the quar
> Of Machiavel; a true Cornelian
> As Tacitus himself, and to be made
> The brooch to any true state-cap in Europe!" I, 1 (401).

But he proves, of course, a caricature, being a mere
puppet in Sir Moth's hands. Like Ateukin, he is dismayed
immediately his position becomes a little dangerous. [1]

(1633)

In the next year (1633) Bishop Morton referred to
the old idea of atheism being Machiavellian: he speaks of

> The women were so fruitfull, that they were
> All got with childe, in compasse of one yeare,
> And that Squire's name, they say, *Belfwagger* was,
> And from that tale, the lying jeere doth passe,
> Wherefore the women there will chide and swagger,
> If any man do aske them for Belfwagger."
> "News from Hell, Hull, Halifax." Spen. Soc. p. 1.

[1] *Bias.*) "Would I were at my shop again,
In court, safe stowed up with my politic bundles."
II, I (409).

"a most barberous fellow, using Machiavelian atheism".
"Discharge." 208.

After a complete silence regarding the Florentine in
the drama of nearly eight years, Heywood revived and
edited Marlowe's "Jew of Malta". In the prologue to the
court he wrote: —

> — "you shall find him still,
> In all his projects, a sound Machiavill;
> And that's his character." (Dyce 142).

Thus, after forty-five years, Heywood could still believe
this awful caricature a "sound Machiavil". The play again
called forth a host of references to the Florentine: but,
whereas half a century before he was mentioned only with
fear and trembling; his name now became in dramatic
literature, after the immediate effect of Marlowe upon
Massinger and Heywood, an object for general ridicule.

In "A New Way to Pay Old Debts" Lady Allworth
says: —

> — "to deceive
> Sir Giles, that's both a lion and a fox
> In his proceedings, were a work beyond
> The strongest undertakers." V, I (Merm. I, 187).

This certainly refers to the "Principe" 18 already in
the drama. No doubt, for the moment Massinger's great
usurer was considered as sound a Machiavel as Marlowe's
was; [1]) but, as we have seen, this usury-idea had been

---

[1]) A certain similarity, unnoticed by critics, exists between
Barabas and Sir Giles: besides being great usurers, each employs his
daughter as a decoy, the latter proving himself more inhuman therein
than the former, for Barabas says to Abigail: —

> "Entertain Lodowick, the governor's son,
> With all the courtesy you can afford,
> Provided that you keep your maiden-head."
>
> II (Dyce 158).

fathered upon the Florentine by the elder dramatist under
the influence of Gentillet. Not without a thought of the
once popular prejudice, did Massinger [1]) term his Machiavellian an atheist:

When Sir Giles goes crazy at the end, Lovell says: —

> "Here is a precedent to teach wicked men,
> That when they leave religion, and turn atheists
> Their own abilities leave them." V, 1 (201).

(1634)

In 1634 William Habington referred *en passant* to the
Florentine, introducing the name into an heroic couplet
as Heywood had just done.

> "The crosse or prosperous fate of Princes, they [courtiers)
> Ascribe to rashnesse, cunning, or delay:
> And on each action comment, with more skill
> Then upon Livy, did old Machavill."
>
> Castara: E. R. 22. p. 96.

Every one must have been struck by Sir Giles' damnable words
to Margaret: —
> "Virgin me no virgins;
> I must have you lose that name, or you lose me.

— — — —

> Give me but proof he has enjoyed thy person." III, 2 (158).

[1]) Ford, strangely associated with Massinger, seems to have known
nothing of Machiavelli: he was the most independent of all the
dramatists; as he says in the prologue to "The Fancies Chaste and
Noble," there is in him —
> "Nothing, but what our author knows his own
> Without a learned theft." Coleridge. 123.

Of Perkin Warbeck he expressly notes: —
> "Famous, and true: most noble, 'cause our own;
> Not forged from Italy, from France, from Spain, —"
>
> (Merm. 381).

In "Love's Sacrifice" mention is made of Dante, Petrarch, Sannazzaro, Ariosto, and Michael Angelo; but Machiavelli remained utterly
unnoticed by Ford.

Sandys used the term as was so often done as a synonym for hypocrite.[1])

Heywood himself naturally felt the effect upon the drama of Marlowe's revived play. In "A Mayden-Head Well Lost" we find: —

(Stroza in Florence fearing the Prince knows Julia's past) —

> "All goes not well, This iugling will be found,
> Then where am I? would I were safe in *Millaine*.
> Here Matchiuell thou wast hatcht: Could not the same
> Planet inspire this pate of mine with some
> Rare stratagem, worthy a lasting character;
> No, 'twill not be: my braine is at a non-plus,
> For I am dull." IV (Vol. IV p. 146).

And indeed Stroza is as "dull" a villain as ever trod the boards: the extent of his stratagems is, as he says to Parma: —

> "I falsely stuft thy head with Jealousies,
> And for some private ends of my revenge,
> Disgrac'd the Generall, and set odds betwixt
> Lauretta and the Princesse: All these mischiefes
> Proceed from my suggestions." IV. (161).

The only Machiavellian traits in him are his egoism,—

Stroza.) "Let Millions fall, so I bee crown'd with rest" IV. (151).

and the device he uses to bring the General into disgrace, and thus ruin him.

But good, old, sentimental Tom's hand must have trembled, when he had screwed his courage up tight enough even to write the name "Matchivell"; and he could not find it in his dear warm heart to let even his most ardent

---

[1]) "Subtle *Machiavelians*, and those which are frequently called the prudent." Essays p. 46.

attempt at a villain go to ruin, and so Stroza is made to repent:[1] —

Stroza.) (when all ends happily)
"Who would strive,
To bee a villaine, when the good thus thrive?" V. (164).

Jonson in his last days sought to adapt his knowledge of Machiavelli to his professional labours. The torso of "The Fall of Mortimer" certainly contains passages, which show the direct influence of the "Principe", though Jonson must also have had Marlowe's Edward II in mind.

Mor.) "There is a fate that flies with towering spirits
Home to the mark, and never checks at conscience.
Poor plodding priests, and preaching friars may make
Their hollow pulpits, and the empty iles
Of churches ring with that round word: but we
That draw the subtile and more piercing air
In that sublimed region of a court,
Know all is good we make so; and go on
Secured by the prosperity of our crimes." (Vol. II, p. 514.)

This is but general Machiavellianism; more specific is this: —

„But I, who am no common-council-man,
Knew injuries of that dark nature done
Were to be throughly done, and not be left
To fear of a revenge: they are light offences
Which admit that: the great ones get above it.
Man doth not nurse a deadlier piece of folly
To his high temper and brave soul, than that
Of fancying goodness, and a scale to live by
So differing from man's life."[2] Ibid.

---

[1] In another play, "The Rape of Lucrece", Heywood used a maxim already in the drama:

Tullia.) (to Tarquin).
"Since you gain nothing by the popular love,
Maintain by fear your princedom." II, 3 (Merm. 354).

[2] Cf. Prin. 3, as before.

and again: —

> "I should think
> When 'mongst a world of bad, none can be good
> (I mean so absolutely good and perfect
> As our religious confessors would have us):
> It is enough we do decline the rumour
> Of doing monstrous things. And yet, if those
> Were of emolument unto our ends,
> Even of those the wise man will make friends,
> For all the brand, and safely do the ill,
> As usurers rob, or our physicians kill." [1) Ibid.

(1636)

In 1636 appeared Dacre's translation of the "Discorsi"; the work is of careful, scholarly sort, and dedicated to James, Duke of Lennox. No doubt, it was wide read.

(1637)

In the next year 1637 Thomas Nabbes in his „Microcosmus" made the time-honored citation of "Machiavelism" for all cunning; but with a tinge of contempt.

> *Melancholy.*) "Not so hot, good Choler. I am partaking, and as discontented at this match [of Physander and Bellanima] as envie can make me. I could hatch a conspiracy to sever them, should cause posterity attribute all Matchiavillianisme to Melancholy."
>
> II (Bullen II, 181).

(1638)

In a tract of the year 1638 [2]), "Killing No Murder" by W. A. and addressed to Cromwell, King Charles is accused, as we have seen Leicester was, of acting under Machiavelli's instructions. [3])

---

[1]) Cf. Prin. XV as before.

[2]) Reprinted 1689.

[3]) "Now in this delineation which I intend to make of a tyrant, all the lineaments, all the colours will be found so naturally to correspond with the life, that it cannot but be doubted, whether his highness be the original or the copy: whether I have, in drawing the

The drama now shows extensively a revived interest in Machiavelli, but his name is no longer feared and soon we find it ridiculed on all sides. Jasper Mayne made a very merry use of it in "The City Match".

Sale.) "You must think a fish like this
May be taught Machiavel,[1]) and made a state-fish."
III, 2 (Dods. 13, 254).

This is said of Timothy Seathrift, whom Captain Quartfield is exhibiting, as "The man-fish — an ocean Centaur".[2])
Thomas Randolf also cited Machiavelli in the jesting vein: —

Chann.) "I'll evidently demonstrate, that of all men
Your carpenters are your best statesmen: of all carpenters
I, being the best, am best of statesmen too.
Imagine, sir, the commonwealth a log

tyrant, represented him; or in representing him expressed a tyrant: and therefore, lest I be expected to deal unsincerely with his highness, and not to have applied these following characters, but made them, I shall not give you any of my own stamping, but such as I find in Plato, Aristotle, Tacitus, and his highness's own evangelist, Machiavel."
Har. Misc. IX, 284.

In the construction of his tyrant Tacitus and Machiavelli get much the better of Plato and Aristotle; the Florentine seems, indeed, to have been carefully studied. One example will suffice. "2. Tyrants accomplish their ends much more by fraud than force: neither virtue nor force, says Machiavel, are so necessary to that purpose, as *una astutia fortunata*, a lucky craft: which, says he, without force has been often found sufficient, but never force without that. And in another place he tells us, their way is *Aggirare i cervelli di gli huomini con astutia*, etc. With cunning plausible pretences to impose upon men's understandings, and in the end they master those that had so little as to rely upon their faith and integrity." Ibid. 290.

[1]) Planché in his excellent "Merchant's Wedding", an amalgamation of this play and Rowley's "Match at Midnight", makes much of this scene, but omits these two lines, since the point would be lost on a modern audience.

[2]) Cf. Southerne "The Disappointment" III, 1 (I, 109)
Alberto) to Clara, commending her subtle licentiousness.
"The policy is true Machiavel, i' faith, on your sides" —

Or a rude block of wood: your statesman comes
(For by that word I mean a carpenter)
And with the saw of policy divides it
Into so many boards or several orders —

— — — —

      Some he carves with titles
Of lord, or knight, or gentleman: some stand plain,
And serve us more for use than ornament:
We call them yeomen (boards now out of fashion):
And, lest the disproportion break the frame,
He with the pegs of amity and concord
As with the glue-pot of good government,
Joints 'em together: makes an absolute edifice
Of the republic. State-skill'd Machiavel
Was certainly a carpenter."
    "The Muses Looking glass" III, 2 (Haz. I, 221).

He likewise satirizes the manner in which would-be
politicians had always been citing their pretended authority.

„*Evion.*) One that, out of an itch to be thought modest, dissembles his
                qualities.
I could, perchance,
Discourse from Adam downward, but what's that
To history? All that I know is only
Th'original, continuance, height, and alteration
Of every commonwealth. I have read nothing
But Plutarch, Livy, Tacitus, Suetonius,
Appian, Dion, Julius, Paterculus.

— — — —

        For modern, I
Have all without the book. Gallo-Bellicus,
Philip de Comines, Machiavel, [1]) Guicciardine,

— — — —

[1]) Cf. 1 Duchess of Newcastle: "The Social Companions"
             II, 1 (12).
 Fullwit.) "I am reading Plutarch's Lives, Thucydides, Machia-
vel, Commincus etc."
 Foote: "The Devil upon Two Sticks"
        I, 1 (Mod. Brit. Dram. V, 378).
 Mary.) "But had you, with me, traced things to their original
source; .... had you read Machiavel, Montesquieu, Locke,

In the Greek I have a smack or so, at
Xenophon, Herodotus, Thucydides, and
Stowes Chronicle." III, 4 (233).

In another play about this time Randolf again made
a facetious reference to Machiavelli.

Dicaeus.) "You [Poverty] can give us field-beds, with
heaven for our canopy, and some charitable stones
for our pillows. We need not expect the felicity of
a horse, to lie at rack and manger; but yet our
asses and we must be content with the same pro-
vender. No roast-beef, no shoulder of mutton, no
cheese-cakes, no Machiavillian Florentines." [1])

"Hey for Honesty" II, 5 (Haz. II, 422).

Shirley also took occasion to use the name as a term
of ridiculous contempt in "The Royal Master". Montalto, a
clumsy villain, denies to the Duke he had defamed
Theodosia: —

Duke.) "Dear Machiavel!
This will not do: the king shall know your stratagems"
IV, 1 (Giff.-Dyce 163).

Montalto is somewhat of a parody on the Machiavellian; Octavio calls him: —

— „that *politician*
Our Protean favourite". I, 1 (110).

He tries to be a dissembler and an egoist, [2]) but is
detected at every point. His Machiavellianism consists in
the time-honored, "delays are fatal", and in the use of

Bacon, Hobbes [etc, etc.] you would have known — woman
is a free agent."

[1]) Nares Glossary ed. Halliwell-Wright p. 317 says: — "Florentine —
a kind of pie .... meat baked in a pie." Cf. Beaumont and Fletcher's
"Woman Hater" X, 1: "custards, tarts, and Florentines."

[2]) *Mont.*)   — "though I thus disguise
My face and tongue, my heart is my own friend,
And cannot wish my ambition supplanted
By any smooth chinn'd prince alive." I, 1 (107).

poison, [1]) which he would make; both of these traits are
parodied, for he never acts, but invariably spoils all by
procrastination, and does not know how to use poison
when he wishes to.

(1639)

In the next year, 1639, Junius made the old cant
reference: —

As our Saviour said, to forewarn all revolters,
"Remember Lot's wife!" so say I, to forewarn all
arch-politicians, and cunning *Machiavelians* of this
world, Remember poor Naboth's vineyard!
"Sin Stigmat." p. 626. apud Johnson-Todd.

In Shirley's "The Politician", Gotharus is an unconscionable villain, [2]) and gives the king one of the old
dramatic Machiavellian advices.

> *Goth.*) „He that aspires hath no religion
> He knows no kindred." III, 1.

Glapthorne in his "Wit in a Constable" speakes of
"Aretines Politicks": [3]) since *L'Unico* never wrote any such
work, this was probably intended for a facetious catch,
like Sylvester's "Mach-Aretine". In Freeman's "Imperiale",
the dastard Spinola exclaims: —

> — "all wickednesse
> Is counted vertue, when 'tis prosperous".

but this may have been self-observation or a reminiscence.

---

[1]) *Mont.*) "There's none but Philoberto conscious
  To my last accusation of the princess;
  Then he must be remov'd: delays are fatal;
  I'll poison him tonight, I have the way." IV, 1 (160).

[2]) *Goth.*) "Let weak statesmen think of conscience,
  I am armed against a thousand stings, and laugh at
  The tales of hell, and other worlds." I, 1.

[3]) Op. cit. I, 1 (Pearson I, 173).

(1640)

Dacres' version of the Principe appeared in 1640, [1]) but it had little or no influence upon the popular prejudice so firmly established: even the translator himself felt it incumbent upon him to excuse the book on the old poison-theory, [2]) so prevalent during the period. But, never the less, this work could not check the tendency to ridicule already well under way in the drama. Habington again referred to the Florentine, not as before with respectful awe, but rather with indifference, in his play, "The Queen of Arragon".

> "First for the plot, it's no way intricate
> By cross deceits in love, nor so high in state,
> That we might have given out in our playbill,
> This day's "The Prince", writ by Nick Machiavil.
>
> — — —· —
>
> No virgin here in breeches casts a mist
> Before her lover's eyes: . . . .
> The language too is easy, such as fell
> Unstudied from his pen: not like a spell
> Big with mysterious words, such as enchant
> The half-witted and confound the ignorant."
>
> Prologue. Dods. XIII, 327.

This irreverent language shows that the old stage traditions, Machiavelli, Tamburlaine's "high astounding terms", even Viola and Belphoebe were passing away.

---

[1]) Ante, p. 2.

[2]) "Poysons are not all of that malignant and noxious quality, that, as destructives of Nature, they are utterly to be abhored: but we find many, nay most of them have their medicinal uses. This book carryes its poyson and malice in it: yet mee thinks the judicious peruser may honestly make use of it in the actions of his life, with advantage."

Preface to Duke of Lennox.

Dacres' "animadversions" are very few, and consist of citations from the Bible, with one exception, where he opposes to Machiavelli's principle of not holding faith, Charles' V famous words in protecting Luther, when urged to break his promise — "Fides rerum promissarum, et si toto mundo exulet, tamen apud imperatorem eam consistere oportet."

As a direct outgrowth of Dacres' translation, however, may be viewed Rawlins' feeble effort to resuscitate the old scare-crow in his "Rebellion". As Ward says, "the villain of the play bears the time-honoured name of Machvile"; [1]) but he bears only the name. The author had merely heard of Machiavelli; certainly, he had never read him, or he would have cited the "fox-and-lion", or "better-be-feared-than-loved" maxim: but no knowledge of the Principe is shown. Nathaniel Richards in his commendatory verses says: —

"Proud daring rebels in their impious way
Of Machiavellian darkness this thy play
Exactly shows." Dods. XIV. p. 5.

Thus to his fellow dramatist, — or rather, fellow dramaticaster, this Count Machvile was a true Machiavellian *redivivus*! Rawlins made a great effort to create a villain, [2])

---

[1]) Ward II, 358.

[2]) *Mach.*) "Heart, wilt not burst with rage, to see these slaves
Fawn like to whelps on young Antonio,
And fly from me as from infection? Death,
Confusion, and the list of all diseases, wait upon your
                lives
Till you be ripe for hell, which when it gapes,
May it devour you all: stay, Machi'vel,
Leave this same idle chat, it becomes woman
That has no strength, but what her tongue
Makes a monopoly; be more a man,
Think, think; in thy brain's mint
Coin all thy thoughts to mischief:
That may act revenge at full.
Plot, plot, tumultuous thoughts, incorporate;
Beget a lump, howe'er deform'd, that may at length,
Like to a cub lick'd by the careful dam,
Become (like to my wishes) perfect vengeance.
Antonio, ay, Antonio — nay, all,
Rather than lose my will, shall headlong fall
Into eternal ruin; my thoughts are high.
Death, sit upon my brow; let every frown
Banish a soul that stops me of a crown." I, 1 (18).

but "the careful dam" evidently did not have saliva enough to lick this "deform'd lump" into a cub. Machvile aspires to the crown, and has Antonio, by his deceit, in a rage innocently kill the Governor; he then becomes Governor himself, plots with the Moorish General Raymond of the French to obtain and share France and Spain, then treacherously has him killed, and is stabbed by him dying. He feigns repentance long enough to kill Antonio, and then dies cursing. [1]) Rawlins was so afraid the audience might forget his villain was a Machiavel, that he calls him a dissembling traitor some twenty odd times, nor can the insipid fool utter a rank sentence without, "Stay Machiavel", "Up Machiavel", or "Hold Machiavel", which he repeats over and over again.

Nabbes again made mention of Machiavelli in another play, "The Unfortunate Mother".

Corvino.)   — for hitherto
    Fortune hath bin my Matchiaveile, [2]) and brought
    Events about I never practis'd for."   V. 3 (Bullen II, 153).

i. e. those who stood in the way of Corvino's ambitious schemes had been removed by chance, as if Fortune were

---

[1]) This is his only traditional Machiavellian trait: such liberality with others' goods as he would make with those of Antonio and Evadne:
         — "his and her goods, to gild
  My lawless doings, I'll give the poor, whose tongues
  Are i' their bellies" III, 1 (47).
is recommended in the "Principe" XVI, but Rawlins would hardly have taken this idea alone from it if the same had been known to him.

[2]) Bullen remarks — "M. whom our old writers regarded as the typical arch-plotter." Cf. Sedley: "The Mulberry Garden" V, 1 (99).
    Everyoung.) (Forecast having been arrested on suspicion.) "This is the happiest accident that ever befel mortal, for an old notorious round-head to be taken for a cavalier at this time: why I ne'er thought it had been in you, this was a stratagem might have become Machiavel himself."

his arch-plotter. Although it is expressly stated in the proeme, [1]) that there is no political treachery in this play, yet the indirect influence of Machiavelli it to be seen in two passages, containing favourite maxims of the dramatic villains. First: the hypocritical-egoistic theory.

Corvino, having hired Cardente to poison Fidelio and the Duchess informs Notho of it: —

> *Notho.*) "Could you have such a conscience?
> *Corv.*) Nice religion
> Awes not a Politician. They both stood
> Betwixt me and my end." V, 1 (148).

Second: the "cut-off-all-accomplices" principle.

Corvino, having raised Notho to the throne, is bidden by him to kill himself for his crimes:

> *Corv.*) "'Tis a command
> Becomes a Prince: and chiefly such a one
> As makes it scruple to preserve his rayser,
> Or to connive at a slight petty sin
> Whose execution hath confirm'd his title." V, 1 (149).

Shirley referred once more to Machiavelli, and this time again with ridicule in "The Constant Maid".

Playfair says of Hornet, after he has been cozened like Mount-Marine in Fletcher's "The Noble gentleman": —

> "Now he looks
> As he did scorn the quorum, and were hungry
> To eat a statesman. 'Las! an office in
> The household is too little for a breakfast;
> A baron, but a morning's draught; he'll gulp it,
> Like a round egg in muscadine. Methinks
> At every wiping of his mouth should drop
> A golden saying of Pythagoras;

---

[1]) "Here is not any glorious Scene of state,

— — — —

No Politician tells his plots unto
Those in the Pit, and what he meanes to do."

A piece of Machiavel[1]) I see already
Hang on his beard, which wants but stroking out:
The statutes, and the Magna Charta, have
Taken a lease at his tongue's end."

IV, 3 (Giff.-Dyce IV, 507).

This is nothing but irreverent mockery; still Shirley clung to some of the traditionary maxims. In "The Imposture" is cited the much-used idea of perjury.

Flav.) — "princes are not
Obliged to keep what their necessities
Contract, but prudently secure their states,
And dear posterity." I, 1 (Giff.-Dyce V, 186).

Again, in "The Doubtful Heir" Leandro says: —

"As great offices, and high
Employments, do expose us to most danger,
They oft teach those possess them a state wisdom;
And by inherent virtues of the place,
Our fear to lose makes us secure ourselves
By art more often, than by conscience." II, 1 (IV, 296).

This sounds as if it might have been taken directly from the "Principe". But most of Shirley's villains, like Beaumont and Fletcher's, are engaged in the same pursuit [2])

---

[1]) Cf. Etherege: "She wou'd if She cou'd" IV, 2 (149).
Freemann (Lady Cockwood having caught him and Courtal with Ariana and Gatty by Mrs. Sentry's stratagem)
"This is Modern *Matchiavil*, I suspect *Courtal*.
Court.) Nay 'tis her Plot doubtless;"
also Cibber: "The Lady's Last Stake" III, 2 (ed. 1760: II, 239).
Lord Wronglove (of Lord George's foolish design upon Miss Notable):
"Faith, 'tis a glorious one — all *Machiavel* was Boys-play to it."

[2]) *Flav.*) "A thousand wheels
Move in my spacious brain whose motions are .
Directed by my ambition, to possess,
And call Fioretta mine; while shallow princes
I make my state decoys, then laugh at them."
"The Imposture." I, 1 (V. 188).

Meyer, Machiavelli.

denounced by Machiavelli; his own idea of political history
seems to have been: —

> "There is no trust to policy or time:
> The things of state are whirl'd by destiny
> To meet their period: art cannot repair them."
>
> Ibid. p. 295.

In an excellent comedy of this year too little known,
"The Knave in Graine New Vampt"[1]), Machiavelli is facetiously reverted to:
Julio, the knave, making Anthonio jealous by a false-
hood, says:

> "I hold with *Machievel*, for fame or profit
> To break oath or league with friend,
> Or Brother; there's nothing gainful bad." II, 1.

But the merry fellow knows no more of Machiavelli
than this, which was a reminiscence of Marlowe, as the
fact, that he is called "Mephistophiles"[2]) and "Faustus".[3])
verifies.

(1641)

By 1641 even the popular non-dramatic literature of
the day began to take this same tone of ridicule: in a tract[1])
attributed to Heywood we find:

---

[1]) "The Knave in Graine New Vampt. A Witty Comedy, Acted
at the *Fortune* many dayes together with great applause. *Written by*
J. D. *Gent* 1640."

[2]) *Pusse.*) "Thou art the very meere *Mephistopholus*" IV, 1.

[3]) *A Country Fellow.*) "He is more than .... a Doctor *Faustus*
or Mephostophilus." V, 1.

[4]) "Machiavel as He lately appeared to his deare Sons, the Mo-
derne Projectors. Divulged for the pretended good of the Kingdomes
of *England*, *Scotland* and *Ireland*." 1641.

Vide: Halkett and Laing: Dic. of Anon. and Pseud. Lit. "Another
copy appeared in the same year, with the title of Machiavel's Ghost as
he appeared —" II, 1531. This tract was probably not by Heywood,
as Hazlitt (Hand-book 366) conjectures, but by Taylor. See Lowndes
III, 1438: also "Cat. of Huth Lib." III, 891.

"Nicolaus Machiavelus Dilectis Filijs suis Projectoribus salutem &c.
And why my dear Off-spring should you feare to fall,

— — — —

Who dares disturbe my Darlings, or compell
Them 'fore their times to take their Thrones in hell,

— — — —

Sweet Sons of Policie, whose glorious traine
Flew like *Minerva* from my *Jove*-like braine;

— — — —

But to incourage you, deare children, looke
On my last Legacy, this little Booke,
Which now emergent from the Presse does shew

— — — —

Your noble qualitie, how just, how true
You are to th' State, what wages you doe pursue
For your owne profits: so deare Sons farewell;
Ere long I hope to welcome you to hell."

Then follows a description of the various projectors:
a specimen [1]) will serve to show there was no use made of
Machiavelli in this prose and poetry pamphlet, the title
being only a catchpenny. So also to this year probably
belongs the undated poem of George Daniel already
mentioned in which Machiavelli is thrice ridiculed: —

"Yet, if a politicke Whisper, beat an Ayre
Upon his Perucke, he [the Discerner] Accosts you bare;

---

[1]) *The Coale Projectors* — Were of a hot constitution, abhor'd
good fires here, because they were sure of a large one hereafter. Their
consciences were like their Coole-pits, deep, and ful of darknesse in
which they desired to continue, for they would admit of no fire-light,
but such as was dearly paid for, fortie shillings a Chaldron being a
charitable price for their farre-fet Fuell: which though deare bought
was hardly good for Ladies: They were meere Salamanders, that though
[they] liv'd by fire themselves could hardly afford it others, having a desire
to reduce the world to a chaos, and make all the yeare winter: But like
Hamaan hang'd on his owne Gallowes, their owne Coales has consum'd
them almost to ashes, and the pit which they digged for others, they
are like to fall into themselves; where we let them rest till they have
cool'd their finger's ends." D. 3.

And gives a formall greeting's cautious Hum
To but Name Machiavel."[1] Idyll 5. (Grosart IV, 230.)

"Formall Politicks
Stood to amuse the world, and bladder out
Light Braines. The Florentine with one Leg Sticks
Keeping the dirty Roode."[2] (Gros. IV, 7.)

"And State-Subverting Magicke has a feate
Beyond all Rule was ever spoken yet.
The Florentine prescribes to duller fooles:
But Stronger flow from all relaxed Soules."
"Hilas and Strephon." (Gros. II, 200).

In another pamphlet[3] of this time even the custom
of calling a dishonest man a Machiavel is denounced as
inappropriate:

---

[1] Cf. "The Loyal Garland" 1686 (Percy Soc. 89. p. 7).
"When our brains well liquor'd are,
Then we charm asleep our care;
Then we account Machevil a fool with his plots,
And cry there's no depth but the bottom o'th' pots."
[2] As Grosart (ibid. 248) remarks, "the allusion is obscure".
[3] "The Atheistical Politician or A Brief Discourse concerning
Nicholas Machiavel." Har. Misc. IV, 441. This is an ingenious defence
of Machiavelli: its object being to brand Strafford and Laud. His vindication is this, — "being to make a grammar for the understanding
of tyrranical government, is he to be blamed for setting down the general rules of such princes. .... Indeed if any can pretend a just
quarrel with Machiavell, they are Kings; for as it is the ordinary course
of light women, to find fault with the broad discource of that they
maintain their power by; so Statesmen may best blame the publication
of these Maximes, ... Yet *Machiavell* saith .... hast thou made thyselfe already an enemie to God and thy people, and hast nothing to
hope for, beyond the honor of this world, therefore to keep thee from
the fury of men be sure thou art perfectly wicked". [It is very interesting to note that this is just what Grillparzer said of the Principe
(Grill. ed. Cotta XVI, 112)] — "the truth is, this man hath raked too
farre in this, which makes him smell as he doth in the nostrils of ignorant people: whereas the better experienced know, it is the wholesome
savour of the court especially when the Prince is of the first head." pp.
4—6 Brit. Mus. Copy dated 1642.

"He, that intends to express a dishonest man, calls him a Machiavillian, when he might as justly say, a Straffordian, or a Cantibirian: we embrace the first apparition of virtue and vice, and let the substance pass by untouched. .... For if we examine the Life of *Lewis* the 11th of *France*, we shall finde he acted more ill, than Machiavill writ, or for ought we know ever thought; yet he hath wisedome inscribed on his Tomb." Brit. Mus. copy, p. 4.

And in the drama of this year — *horribile dictu* the ingratitude of humanity! — he, whose awful name had for so long made the cold shivers run down the audience's back, even he is called an ass: — "but, masters, remember, that I am an ass. .... Bring him away. O, that I had been writ down an ass!" —

Agathocles (of Mazares): —
 "Machiavel, thou art an ass,[1]) a very ass to him" (aside).
 Tatham: "The Distracted State". I, 1 (Dram. of Res. I, 46).

And this is doubly insulting, for Mazares is a very weak villain: his only policy to preserve himself and his empire from ruin is, — to commit suicide! Never-the-less, in the play itself occur again and again [2]) two of the time-honored maxims; to make away with accomplices and to use deception. As Cleander says of him:

   Silly ass!
 That only art employed to carry me
 Unto my bliss, thyself unto destruction!
 He's held an animal has no deceit
 In these times to make his own fortune great." V, 1 (88).

---

 [1]) Cf. Settle: "A Narrative" p. 5.
— "how sillily and awkwardly these asses, these Matchiavils put their Noddles together."
 [2]) Five different tyrants usurp the crown in succession by deceit, (Mazares, Archias, Cleander, Agathocles, and Antanter), and each would be rid of his respective councillor and right hand man. Tatham says the play was written in 1641: it was published (remodelled?) in 1651 as the editor says against Cromwell. Intro. 35.

After having called poor old Machiavel an ass, there was nothing left now but to most ignominiously shuffle him off the stage. And so in Marmion's "Antiquary", Bravo, Aurelio's noble father, disguised as a malcontent, thus, dismisses him: —

> "Well, go thy ways, old Nick Machiavel, there will never be the peer of thee for wholsome policy and good counsel. Thou took'st pains to chalk men out the dark paths and hidden plots of murther and deceit, and no man has the grace to follow thee: the age is unthankful, thy principles are quite forsaken and worn out of memory."
>
> III. (Dods. XIII, 458.)

And indeed "old Nick Machiavel" did "go his ways" off the stage and out of dramatic literature, in which we hear no more of him for ten years. At this point, the discussion on hand practically ends; the theatres were closed Sept. 2 nd 1642 and the drama, though not dead, became torpid, to say the least, until its re-awakening at the Restoration. For the sake of clearing up one or two points, however, it seems advisable to continue the research to the death of Shirley in 1666.

(1642)

In the next year (1642) Machiavelli can be mentioned without the least aspersion.

> "Touching Commines, who was contemporary with *Machiavel*, 'twas a witty speach of the last Queen Mother of *France, that he made more Heretiques in Policy, than* Luther *ever did in Religion.* James Howell: "Instructions for Forreine Travell". Arber 16 p. 23.

The mere name was again used as a catch-penny title, [1]) which runs, "A Machavillian Plot, or A Caution for

---

[1]) This was often done later. See Allibone II, 1171: "The Craftsman". Oct. 5, 1734. In 1683, "Matchiavel Junior".

England". This was a tract urging the King to build
fortresses[1]) and was issued to feed the animosity against
Charles in 1642.

Sir Thomas Browne also alluded to Machiavelli this
year in his "Christian Morals".

"Though I have no great opinion of Machiavel's
learning, yet I shall not presently say that he was
but a novice in Roman history, because he was
mistaken in placing Commodus after the Emperor
Severus." [2])

Saintsbury "Hist. Eliz. Lit." 341. (Wilkin IV, 81.)

(1644)

Taylor as late as 1644 still held tenaciously on to the
old tradition, citing Machiavelli as in the devil's pay.

"First you (Maister *John Booker)* threaten us, that
John Pym's ghost shall haunt us, and hunt us out of
Oxford Short-lye, but this your Short-lye is a Long-
lye, a Broad-lye and a Round-lye. For we at *Oxford*
doe know the Ghosts of all such Pestiferous Rebels to
be attendants upon their old maister, and receiving
their wages with *Achitophel,* [3]) *Machiavell etc.*" —

"No Mercurius Aulicus" (p. 3 Spen. Soc. 2 nd Col.).

---

[1]) Cf. Gentillet III, 33 and Prin. XX. Arte d. Guer. VII (396):
Disc. II, 24 (268). There is not a word about Machiavelli, except in
the title; but the piratical publisher remembered either from Gentillet or
the Florentine himself, that this building of fortresses had been discussed in the "Principe":

[2]) Later on, Browne condemned Machiavelli's bold attack upon
Christian humility:

"We applaud not the judgement of Machiavel, that Christianity
makes men cowards". Hydriotaphia (Wilkin III, 487).

[3]) Cf. "The Badger in the Fox-Trap". (Scott in Dryden IX, 200)
where is said of Shaftesbury:

"Besides, my titles are as numerous
As all my actions various, still, and humerous.
Some call me Tory, some Achitophel,
Some Jack-a-Dandy, some old Machiavel."

Francis Quarles also used, or made reference to a use of Machiavelli in the old way. [1])

(1645)

The popular literary hack Taylor never got out of the old rut: thus in "A Letter sent to London from a Spie at Oxford" [2]) we find: —

"You, M. *Pym,* have made your wisedome perspicuously famous, You have outdone the *Roman Cataline,* You have overmatched old *Nicholas Machiavil* the *Florentine,* and renowned Guido will be forgot." —

(1647)

In a ballad of the year 1647 an author, (Sir Francis Wortley?), thought it more apposite to term hypocritic

---

Dryden never cites Machiavelli: in the "Essay upon Satire" fathered upon him, it is written of Shaftesbury: —
"As by our little Machiavel we find,
    That nimblest creature of the busy kind." Ibid. XV, 208.
See also "Oceana and Britannia" wrongly attributed to Marvel: —
    — "a reverend sire appears,

— — — —

His name I ask'd; he said, Politico,
Decended from the divine Nicolo."
                                    Marvell ed. Gros. I, 446.

[1]) *"Dr. Burges:* .... Again, let such as be zealous sticklers for Democraticall, or Aristocraticall discipline, consider how ill the Church can be governed by one policy, and the Commonwealth by another. *Cal.*[umniator] Our Doctor is grown a *Machiavilian,* and forgets that Piety is the best *Policy."* "The Whipper Whipt." (Grosart I, 166.)
    Another example in "Hell's Hurlie-Burlie", where the Devil says of the Pope: —
    "This Machiavell far exceeded us in wickednesse." p. 3.
    [2]) Grey in Butler (240) says this was in 1643, but the Brit. Mus. copies are all of 1645. Grey also says: — "It is observed by a spy at Oxford, to Pym 1643 .... That they [sic! which they?] have overmatched old Nicholas Machiavel." — Nothing of the kind is observed. Taylor is denouncing Pym. — Taylor's pun is the time-honored one; this linking of Cataline and Machiavel is interesting à propos of "Henry VI."

villains "Jews of Malta", than by the old cant word
"Machiavellians": this is peculiarly interesting; he evidently
saw the absurdity of the old tradition, and also what had
given rise to it: i. e. Marlowe's Jew.

> "But, oh! these subtle men [1]) must not
> (Above all others) be forgot,
> We Jewes of Malta call;
> Who lately have a new trick found,
> To make men for their owne compound; —
> These get the Devill and all."
> Polit. Ballads ed. Wright (Percy Soc. p. 28).

In this year also was made a translation of Belphegor. [2])

(1649)

It is surprising, that Machiavelli was so seldom cited
in popular literature by the Loyalists against the Cromwellists
and *vice versa*. It must be concluded, the name no longer
possessed the charm it once had. But one case was noted
in 1649. Charles we have already seen denounced as a
Machiavellian; this time the same is said of Cromwell:

> "'Tis high contempt not for to Fast and pray,
> And hold as blest Saint *Cromwel's* Holy day,

---

[1]) In another place is said of them:
"To hate all good and hugge all evill,
In an angel's shape to outact the Devill,
With all kinds of baseness to comply,
And make the whole realm a monopoly,
To laugh at conscience
And be quite void of sence,
Now church and state they've in pieces rent,
To breake all kind of trust,
And to do nothing that is just,
Are some priviledges of this Parliament." Ibid. 22.

[2]) "The Devil a Married Man, or the devill hath met with his
Match. 1647." It may as well be stated here as elsewhere that the
writer found in the Brit. Mus. an excellent versification (hitherto apparently unknown to scholars) of Machiavelli's novelette called "Hell upon
Earth, or the Devil tir'd with Matrimony. London 1718."

The Devils a saint, if he deserves to be
One for his Machivillian Treacherie."
                    "The Loyall Subjects Jubilee" p. 56.

(1651)

Taylor, who never tired of the once popular catch-word, brought it in as usual in 1651:

"Some man ere hee'd be cal'd a Puritan,
Will turne a damned Machiavilian,
A Libertine, Papist, or else what not?
To keep his name from so impure a blot."

(1652)

After an almost complete silence of seven years appeared a pamphlet, "Modern Policies, taken from Machiavel, Borgia, and other choice Authors, by an eye-witnesse". In the "Epistle Dedicatorie" we read: —

"It does to me a little relish of Paradox, that wher-ever I come, Machiavill is verbally curs'd and damn'd, and yet practically imbrac'd and asserted."

Then follow ten maxims, given and refuted or denied, [1]) just as in Gentillet, which the author certainly had before him either in the original or in Patericke's translation. This refutation may have revived some interest in its subject; at any rate in this same year mention was again made of Machiavelli in the drama after a long silence. [2]) Cosmo Manuche in his "Loyall Lovers" cited him somewhat in the old way.

Gripeman, (when he learns his daughter Letesia lost and is denounced by Sent-well), cries:

---

[1]) E. g. "Machiavel .... advised .... The Polititian must have the shadow of Religion, but the substance hurts. .... Colasterion: But let all sober Christians know, that this shell of Religion, though it may be of external conducement, yet there is nothing that God's pure and undeluded eye looks on with more abhorency." p. 7.

[2]) To be sure, but few plays were written between 1642 and 1660.

> "O my brains, my brains.
> Great *Lucifer*, I do conjure thee, summon *Boniface*,
> *Mahomet*, *Copernicus*, *Matchiavil*, *Ecphantus*,
> and all thy learned Polliticians in thy black *Caos* to invent a
> torment (yet unheard of) to inflict upon this slave." IV, 1 (41).

(1653)

In the next year Shirley once more referred to the religious-hypocrisy principle: —

Mendoza.)   — "but duty and religion
> Are handsome visors to abuse weak sight,
> That cannot penetrate beyond the bark,
> And false complection of things."
>   "The Court Secret" IV, 3 (Giff.-Dyce V, 2194).

(1654)

In 1654 Whitlocke referred *en passant* to "Machiavells" in the old manner:
> "But all the Machiavells on this little Turfe, ...
> I can silence with that oraculous, ingenious Apologie
> of my Lord *Bacon*."
>   "Zoötomia" p. 178 apud Fennel: Stand. Dic.

(1656)

Two years later appeared "A Discourse upon Nicholas Machiavel: or, An impartial examination of the justnesse of the censure commonly laid upon him." It was merely a second enlarged edition of a previous tract.[1] The author added here, what has often been intoned since, and what gave rise to much of the Elizabethan "scare": the injustice of considering the "Principe" alone without regarding Machiavelli's other works: —

---

[1] "The Atheistical Politician" — (ante p. 164); it appeared a third time as "The Vindication of that Hero of Political Learning, Nicholas Machiavel, The Second Tacitus," by James Boevey Aetatis 71. 1692, Har. Misc. X, 183. He was, of course, the author of all three editions under separate titles.

"He was Secretary to the State of Florence, [sic!] of which he hath left an incomparable *History*, with other Bookes; so full of Truth, Learning and Experience, that the hand of Detraction hath not been able to asperse them; onely it endeavours to attack some stragling expressions in a small Pamphlett, called his *Prince*, which are with farre lesse charity remembered, than so many larger and better pieces forgotten." p. 121.

(1657)

In the next year (1657) was published a second edition of the "Modern Policies". [1])

The idea of ridiculing Machiavelli, so marked in the last years of his real stage existence, was now revived for the last time in the drama of the period under discussion by Aston Cokaine in "Trapolin Creduto Principe: or Trappolin suppos'd a Prince". Among the Dram. Pers. are found:

Barberino.⎫ two noble Florentines. [2])
Machavil. ⎭

Ward [3]) remarks on this play, — "It will interest those who like to note the vitality of dramatic traditions to observe that the Duke of Florence in Cokaine's piece, during whose absence the sham Duke plays his pranks, leaves behind him as one of his lieutenants "the lord Machavil", "one of those that doth in Florence nourish vice". Now we have seen that the vitality of this dramatic tradition had been sapped very dry some eighteen years previous, when it was ridiculed on all sides; but the historian of English Dramatic Literature had not observed

[1]) Ante p. 170. This 2nd ed. is signed "W. Blois".
[2]) In Tate's alteration (1685) the name Machavil was changed to Alberto, the point of the parody being no longer perspicuous: the latter was retained also in the *rifacimenti* of Drury (1732), of Ramsay (1733), and in that of 1818.
[3]) II, 450.

this fact. Nor has he been felicitous in his appliccation of the above quotation. For if we consider the phrase — "one of those that doth in Florence nourish vice" — we shall find that it, is spoken not of Machavil at all, but of Trappolin by Barbarino to Machavil as the citation shows.

Barberino and Machavil have been left in charge of Florence during the Duke's abscence: the former has had Trappolin arrested:

"*Enter* Barbarino, Machavil, Mattemores, *and* Officers, *leading* Trappolin *after them.*

Bar.) This man, Lord Machavil, is one of those
    That doth in Florence nourish vice: he is
    A pander, — one that, if he sees a stranger,
    Straight makes acquaintance with him, for what end
    Yourself may guess. So he may gain thereby,
    He would betray our daughters, lead our sons
    To brothels, vicious and full of rottenness.
Tra.) I wonder how the devil he came to know anything that I did.
Bar.) This writing yesternight was presented to me.
    Here you may see what enormities he is guilty of.
Tra.) His lordship would show himself a great hater of bawdry.
Mac.) 'Tis good we did examine him." I, 2 (Dram. of Rest. 128).

Machavil does anything but "nourish vice", he is simply a parody on the Florentine Statesman. This caricature proves conclusively, what has before been seen, that the view taken of Machiavelli had changed from awful reverence to irreverent ridicule — from one extreme to the other.

In this play Machavil and Barberino are merely the puppets with which Trappolin, charmed into the Duke's shape by his "natural father", Mago the magician, makes the fun of the play.

There is not one word of Machiavellianism in the play, and "wise Machavil", as the real Duke sarcastically calls him, is made sport of at every turn. Let this suffice:

Barbarino wishes to punish Trappolin for pandarism;
Machavil tries him: —

Mac.) "Ere we come to this pandarism, I'll examine him about other
matters. Sir, do you never use to carry pistols about you?
Tra.) Sometimes, and please your excellence, I do.
Bar.) Write down that, notary.
Tra.) What does your lordship mean? I did not steal them.
Mac.) I know well enough what I do. Sirrah! you want to shoot
somebody.
Tra.) Beseech your honour to take me along with you: I mean
money.
Mac.) That's vain! then, notary, tear it out.
Bar.) Do you ne'er carry other arms neither?
Tra.) Many times, my lord.
Bar.) Notary, down with it! he shall be talk'd with for that.
Tra.) Your honour is deceiv'd again: I meant only arms upon seals,
or scutcheons from heralds.
Mac.) This is nothing, notary: tear it out!" I, 2 (128).

This is bad enough and degenerates into horse-play
in II, 3 (150), where Trappolin supposed the prince calls: —
„Sirrah Barberino! hold by Mach's breeches, and
stoop, for on thy back will I ride to my palace."
and thus Trappolin rides to the Duke's palace on the very
men who had banished him.

More need not be said to prove this a parody on the
man with whose works Cokaine was acquainted as he himself states elsewhere. [1]

(1658)

In the next year (1658) Cowley made a facetious use

---

[1] "It appears that Cotton's library contained some of the best
Italian authors, as Cokayne says in one of his effusions, —
D'Avila, Bentivoglio, Guicciardine,
And Machiavil the subtle Florentine,
In their originals, I have read through,
Thanks to your library and unto you:
The prime historians of late times; at least,
In the Italian tongue allow'd the best."
"Walton and Cotton's Complete Angler", ed. Nicholas CLXVI.

of the Florentine's reputation for craft in his "Cutter of Colman Street".

Puny says to Aurelia after she has outwitted him into marrying her instead of Lucia:

> "I'll out: Uncle Father your Blessing — my little
> *Matchiavil*, I knew well enough 'twas you: What
> did you think I knew not Cross from Pile."

V, 13 (ed. 1721: p. 827).

This was but a reminiscence of the grand old drama, of Jonson [1]) and Marlowe [2]), to whom Cowley's genius looked back with longing eyes.

(1659)

In 1659 was published "My Lord Whitlock's Reports on Machiavil: or his recollections for the use of Students of Modern policy". This was simply a lampoon on Whitlocke, in which Machiavelli was neither mentioned nor used, except in the title as a jest.

(1660)

In a broadside of the next year the old ideas were again brought to light: —

> "One [Gen. Monck] that is verst in honest politics,
> And deeply hateth such pedantick tricks
> As Murder, Rapine, Perjury, which crimes
> Were in vile Cromwel's and the Rumper's times

---

[1]) Jonson was the first to call a woman a Mach. *V. ante*, p. 89. Cf. the popular catch of a later day.

> "All the subtle lime twigs laid
> By Machiavel, the waiting maid;"

also Addison in Spectator 561.

[2]) Marlowe's heroes are often referred to:

e. g. *Puny*) — "but I'm the very *Jew* of *Malta*, if she [Aurelia] did not use me since that, worse than I'd use a rotten apple." II, 4 (762).

Again: Puny calls this same Aurelia (the "little Matchiavil" of V, 13)

> — "that little Mephostophilus." III, 2 (787).

Accounted godliness, and in wrong sense
Stil'd acts of Heaven's gracious Providence:
But now (I hope) we shall be freed from th' Spell
And witching Charms o' th' Devill and Machiavel.
They must invent new sleights, a cloak that's stronger,
Religion will vayle vileny no longer:
All men have found their false knavery out,
But noble George hath put them to the rout."
"The Entertainment of Lady Monk at Fisher's Folly."
Collier:[1]) Illus. II, 33.

In this year was printed a drama, "The Faithful
Friends", doubtfully ascribed to Beaumont and Fletcher.
It is full of gross anachronisms;[2]) in it Marcus Tullius
says of King Titus Martius, supposing him the author of
Rufinus' plan for his betrayal and murder: —

"And let us study how to be revenged
On this injurious king, King Machiavel." IV, 1 (Darley 546).

The king's villainy, like that of most of Beaumont and
Fletcher's kings, is seeking to prostitute a subject's wife,
and was denounced as fatal in the "Principe". Rufinus
is an arch-villain; his daring scheme to have Marcus killed
and Rome betrayed to ease his petty jealousy, out-Machiavels even Elizabethan Machiavels.

(1661)
Cowley, about 1661 in his "Discourse concerning the
Government of Oliver Cromwell",[3]) referred to Machiavelli,

---

[1]) This passage contains the old ideas, and is unique in containing
them at so late a date; the poems appeared first in Collier's "Illustrations of Early Eng. Pop. Lit." — "from original Broadsides in the
editor's possession, and he knows of no other copies of them." *Verbum
sapienti.*

[2]) E. g. Pergamus, hanging up his arms in Mars' temple, speaks
of John of Gaunt and Guildhall thousands of years before they were
in existence.

[3]) In the same tract Cowley mentioned him again à propos of
Cataline, which is interesting for Henry VI.
"And since I happen here to propose Cataline .... give me
leave to transcribe the character which Cicero gives of this

but again displayed the influence Marlowe - Gentillet had
upon him by mixing up the idea of his teaching how to
"get riches" with that of obtaining the "supreme place".

The spirit of Cromwell says: — „I am glad you
allowe me at least artful dissimulation and un-
wearied diligence in my hero; and I assure you that
he whose life is constantly drawn by those two
shall never be misled out of the way of greatness
.... Was ever riches gotten by your golden medio-
crities? or the supreme place attained to by virtues
that must not stir out of the midde? Do you study
Aristotle's politics, and write, if you please, comments
upon them: and let another but practice Machiavel: [1])
and let us see then which of you two will come to
the greatest preferment." Chalmers VII, 185.

(1663)

One more reference in non-dramatic literature remains
to be discussed. Butler in his "Hudibras" has these
lines: —

> "Nick Machiavel had ne'er a trick,
> (Though he gave name to our old Nick.)
> But was below the least of these", [of the Cavaliers].
> Chandos Classics p. 240.

As Grey remarks: —
„Warburton is of the opinion, that this is a blunder
of the editor [2]) to suppose the devil was called
Old Nick, from Nick Machiavel the Florentine (but
it was certainly the mistake of the author, who
continued it in every edition of his life) who lived

---

noble slave, because it is a general description of all ambitious men, and which Machiavel perhaps would say ought
to be the rule of their life and actions." Ibid. 187.

[1]) *Ante* p. 87 note 3.

[2]) See Todd in Johnson's Dic. 1827 *sub* Nick.

in the 16th century; whereas they could not but
know, that our English writers before Machiavelli's
time, used the word Old Nick very commonly to
signify the devil: that it came from our Saxon an-
cestors .... and [Warburton] thinks that

"He gave aim to our Old Nick,"

which has a great deal of humour and satire in it,
as supposing Machiavel to be so consummate a
politician as to read lectures to the devil himself,
would be an emendation."

All the numerous editors of "Hudibras" have had their
say on this passage. Warburton's supposition is as far-
fetched and nonsensical as Malone's idea about Marlowe
and Kett. The truth is, this was merely a facetious jest
of Butler, who certainly knew better, but indulged freely
in poetic license. [1]) That it was often taken for earnest
the following lines prove from a later poem:

"In this prodigal trick, They have outdone Old Nick;
For what he did, he did show

---

[1]) See Bohn: "Hudibras" II, 314. "When Machiavelli is represented
as such a proficient in wickedness, that his name hath become an appel-
lation for the devil himself, we are not less entertained by the smartness
of the sentiment, than we should be if it were supported by the truth
of history. By the same kind of poetical license Empedocles, in the
second canto, is humorously said to have been acquainted with the writings of Alexander Ross, who did not live till about 2000 years after
him." It is interesting to compare with Butler what "The Free Bri-
ton" (Oct. 10, 1734) says of a letter, called "Nick. Machiavel to Caleb
D'anvers," after bespeaking it "hellish": —

— "we must own it to be Nick's, but not Machiavel's."
Gents. Mag. IV, 538.

Macaulay in his essay actually took Butler's jest in earnest; the
"Nation" of Oct. 22, 1891 seems also seriously to regard Machiavelli as
"Old Nick".

"The army of his [Machiavelli's] enemies, ... holding fast to
their detestation of "Old Nick".

There title is the same, And so is ther aim
For aught any man doth know."

Butler himself refers several times to Machiavelli in
the regular cant way:

"There is a Machiavilian [1]) plot (Tho' ev'ry *nare olfact* it not)
And deep design in't [The Solemn League] to divide
The well-affected that confide,
By setting brother against brother,
To claw and curry one another." Ibid. 48.

The drama made but two more mentions of Machiavelli before Shirley's death: in Richard Head's "Hic et
Ubique" he is ridiculed as he was back in the period just
before the closing of the theatres.

Half-witted Contriver, with his "ingenious plots", —
for draining the bogs of Ireland to find vast quantities of
gold etc. etc. says of himself, when Thrivewell intimates
he will adopt him: —

"I am now clearly of the belief, my Mother's imagination was fixt on *Oliver* or *Mazerin*, when she con-
ceiv'd me, or that she long'd to eat five or six leaves
of *Machiavel's* politick Discourses." IV, 2 (45).

(1664)

In one of the two plays of Killegrew that were ever
acted, in "The Parson's Wedding", we find:

Captain.) „Yes, faith, it was my plot, and I glory in't;
to undermine my Machiavel, which so greedily
swallowed that sweet bait that had this hook."
IV, 2 (Dods. XIV, 483).

This is merely the cant word used of the Parson who
tried to outwit the speaker, but was overreached by "the
Captain and his Wanton". Thus to designate a shrewd,

---

[1]) In "The Court Burlesqued", Carry is called a "cunning Machiavilian cuff", (p. 179) and in "Mola Asinaria" Butler speaks of "Machiavilian tricks". (p. 305).

or a would-be shrewd person [1]) became quite popular in the post-Restoration drama.

---

[1]) Cf. Murphy: "The Way to Keep Him". II, 2 (Mod. Brit. Dram. IV, 402):

> *Sir Bashful Constant.*) "I wear admirably well, Mr. Lovemore.
> *Love.*) Do you!
> *Sir B.*) As young as ever: but I don't let her [Lady Constant] know it.
> *Love.*) Well: If you are discreet in that point, you are a very Machiavel."

Vide ante: Congreve, Farquhar, Etherege, etc. etc.

Cf. Sheridan, "The Duenna" II, 3:

> *Isaac.*) "I'm a Machiavel, a very Machiavel."

tolerance and understanding, I thank my sister, Shelagh, and brother, Michael; my paternal cousins, Anna and Patrick Whitley; and my half-brother, John Leuthold. Finally, I thank my partner, Katy Petre, whose constancy, generosity, and love saw me through my best and worst moments.

=

Audio-visual material related to *What Disturbs Our Blood* accessible at: www.jamesfitzgerald.info

SELECT BIBLIOGRAPHY AND SOURCES

BOOKS:

Akenson, Donald Harman. *The Irish in Ontario: A Study in Rural History*. Ist ed. Montreal: McGill-Queen's University Press, 1984.

Andre, Linda. *Doctors of Deception: What They Don't Want You to Know About Shock Treatment*. New Jersey: Rutgers University Press, 2009.

Ardagh, John. *Ireland and the Irish: Portrait of a Changing Society*. London: Penguin Group, 1995.

Barry, John M. *The Great Influenza: The Epic Story of the Deadliest Plague in History*. New York: Penguin Group USA, 2004.

Bator, Paul and Andrew Rhodes. *Within Reach of Everyone: A History of the University of Toronto School of Hygiene and the Connaught Laboratories*. 2 vols. Ottawa: Canadian Public Health Association, 1990, 1995.

Beers, Clifford W. *A Mind That Found Itself.* Pittsburgh: University of Pittsburgh Press, 1981.

Best, Henry B. M. *Margaret and Charley: The Personal Story of Dr. Charles Best, The Co-Discoverer of Insulin*. Toronto: The Dundurn Group, 2003.

Blair, John S. G. *In arduis fidelis: Centenary History of the Royal Army Medical Corps 1898–1998*. Edinburgh: Scottish Academic Press Ltd., 1998.

Bliss, Michael. *The Discovery of Insulin*. Chicago: University of Chicago Press, 1982.

———. *Banting: A Biography.* Toronto: University of Toronto Press, 1984.

———. *William Osler: A Life in Medicine*. Toronto: Oxford University Press, 1999.

Braceland, Francis J. *The Institute of Living: The Hartford Retreat, 1822–1972*. Connecticut: Hartford, 1972.

Breggin, Peter. *Toxic Psychiatry: Why Therapy, Empathy, and Love Must Replace the Drugs, Electroshock, and Biochemical Theories of the "New Psychiatry."* New York: St. Martin's Press, 1991.

Brome, Vincent. *Ernest Jones: A Biography*. New York: W. W. Norton & Company, 1983.

Bryer, Jackson and Cathy W. Barks, eds. *Dear Scott, Dearest Zelda: The Love Letters of F. Scott and Zelda Fitzgerald*. London: Bloomsbury Publishing PLC, 2002.

Buchan, William. *John Buchan: A Memoir*. London: Buchan & Enright Publishers Ltd, 1982.

Bulfinch, Thomas. *Bulfinch's Mythology*. New York: Avenel Books, 1979.

Burlingame, Clarence Charles. *A Psychiatrist Speaks: The Writings and Lectures of Dr. C. Charles Burlingame, 1885–1950*. 1959.

Cassel, Jay. *The Secret Plague: Venereal Disease in Canada, 1838–1939*. Toronto: University of Toronto Press, 1987.

Chernow, Ron. *Titan: The Life of John D. Rockefeller, Sr.* New York: Vintage, 1997.

Connor, J. T. H. *Doing Good: The Life of Toronto's General Hospital*. Toronto: University of Toronto Press, 2000.

Cooter, Roger, Mark Harrison, and Steve Sturdy, eds. *Medicine and Modern Warfare*. Amsterdam: Editions Rodopi B. V., 1999.

Cosbie, Waring Gerald. *The Toronto General Hospital, 1819–1965: A Chronicle*. Toronto: MacMillan of Canada, 1975.

Dain, Norman. *Clifford W. Beers: Advocate for the Insane*. Pittsburgh: University of Pittsburgh Press, 1980.

Davenport-Hines, Richard. *The Pursuit of Oblivion: A Global History of Narcotics 1500–2000*. New York: W. W. Norton & Company, 2002.

Davies, T. G. *Ernest Jones, 1879–1958*. Cardiff: University of Wales Press, 1979.

Debré, Patrice. *Louis Pasteur*. Baltimore: The Johns Hopkins University Press, 1994.

Defries, Robert Davies. *The First Forty Years, 1914–1955: Connaught Medical Research Laboratories.* Toronto: University of Toronto Press, 1968.

de Kruif, Paul. *Microbe Hunters.* New York: Harcourt, Brace and Co., 1926.

Dowbiggin, Ian Robert. *Keeping America Sane: Psychiatry and Eugenics in the United States and Canada, 1880–1940.* Ithaca, NY: Cornell University Press, 1997.

Duffin, Jacelyn. *History of Medicine: A Scandalously Short Introduction.* Toronto: University of Toronto Press, 1999.

El-Hai, Jack. *The Lobotomist: A Maverick Medical Genius and His Tragic Quest to Rid the World of Mental Illness.* Hoboken: John Wiley & Sons, Inc., 2005.

Farley, John. *To Cast Out Disease: A History of the International Health Division of the Rockefeller Foundation (1913–1951).* New York: Oxford University Press, 2003.

Fedunkiw, Marianne. *Rockefeller Foundation Funding and Medical Education in Toronto, Montreal, and Halifax.* Montreal: McGill-Queen's University Press, 2005.

FitzGerald, John G. *An Introduction To The Practice of Preventive Medicine.* St. Louis: The C. V. Mosby Company, 1922.

Forbush, Byron and Bliss Forbush. *Gatehouse: The Evolution of the Sheppard and Enoch Pratt Hospital, 1853–1986: A History.* Philadelphia: J. B. Lippincott Company, 1986.

Frank, Leonard Roy. *The History of Shock Treatment.* 1978.

Frayn, Douglas H. *The Clarke and Its Founders: The Thirtieth Anniversary: A Retrospective Look at the Impossible Dream.* Toronto: The Clarke Monograph Series, No. 6, 1996.

———. *Psychoanalysis in Toronto: Historical Perspectives.* Toronto: Ash Productions, 2000.

Friedland, Martin. *The University of Toronto: A History.* Toronto: University of Toronto Press, 2002.

Gamwell, Lynn and Nancy Tomes. *Madness in America: Cultural and Medical Perceptions of Mental Illness Before 1914.* Ithaca: Cornell University Press, 1995.

Geison, Gerald. *The Private Science of Louis Pasteur*. Princeton: Princeton University Press, 1995.

Griffin, John D. *In Search of Sanity: A Chronicle of the Canadian Mental Health Association, 1918–1998*. London (ON): Third Eye Publications, 1989.

Grosskurth, Phyllis. *The Secret Ring: Freud's Inner Circle and the Politics of Psychoanalysis*. New York: Addison-Wesley, 1991.

Hare, Ronald. *The Birth of Penicillin and the Disarming of Microbes*. London: Allen & Unwin, 1970.

Harris, Seale. *Banting's Miracle: The Story of the Discoverer of Insulin*. Philadelphia: J. B. Lippincott Company, 1946.

Hincks, Clare. *Prospecting For Mental Health: The Autobiography of Clare Hincks*. Unpublished, 1962.

Hurd, Henry Mills. *The Institutional Care of the Insane in the United States and Canada*. Baltimore: The Johns Hopkins University Press, 1917.

Jackson, A.Y. *Banting as an Artist*. Toronto: Ryerson Press, 1943.

Jonas, Gerald. *The Circuit Riders: Rockefeller Money and the Rise of Modern Science*. New York: W. W. Norton & Company, 1989.

Jones, Ernest. *Free Associations: Memories of a Psychoanalyst*. London: Hogarth, 1959.

Karlen, Arno. *Man and Microbes*. New York: Tarcher (Penguin Group USA), 1995.

Kerr, Robert and Douglas Waugh. *Duncan Graham: Medical Reformer and Educator*. Toronto: The Dundurn Group, 1989.

Kolata, Gina. *Flu: The Story of the Great Influenza Pandemic of 1918 and the Search for the Virus That Caused It*. New York: Farrar, Straus and Giroux, 1999.

Leavitt, Judith Walzer. *Typhoid Mary: Captive to the Public's Health*. New York: Putnam Publishing Group, 1996.

Levine, Israel E. *The Discoverer of Insulin: Dr. Frederick G. Banting*. New York: Julian Messner, 1959.

Lifton, Robert Jay. *The Nazi Doctors: Medical Killing and the Psychology of Genocide*. New York: Basic Books, 1986.

Lownie, Andrew. *John Buchan: The Presbyterian Cavalier*. Edinburgh:

Canongate Books, 1995.

MacDougall, Heather. *Activists and Advocates: Toronto's Health Department, 1883–1963*. Toronto: The Dundurn Group, 1990.

Maddox, Brenda. *Freud's Wizard: The Enigma of Ernest Jones*. London: John Murray, 2006.

McLaren, Angus. *Our Own Master Race: Eugenics in Canada 1885–1940*. Toronto: University of Toronto Press, 1990.

Montagnes, Ian. *An Uncommon Fellowship: The Story of Hart House*. Toronto: University of Toronto Press, 1969.

Nikiforuk, Andrew. *The Fourth Horseman: A Short History of Plagues, Scourges, and Emerging Viruses*. Toronto: Penguin Group, 1991.

O'Brien, John. *The Vanishing Irish: The Enigma of the Modern World*. New York: McGraw-Hill, 1953

O'Driscoll, Robert and Lorna Reynolds, ed. *The Untold Story: The Irish In Canada*. 2 vols. Toronto: Celtic Arts of Canada, 1988.

Oliver, Wade W. *The Man Who Lived for Tomorrow: A Biography of William Hallock Park*. New York: E. P. Dutton, 1941.

Oppenheim, Janet. *Shattered Nerves: Doctors, Patients, and Depression in Victorian England*. New York: Oxford University Press, 1991.

Parkin, Alan. *A History of Psychoanalysis in Canada*. Toronto: Toronto Psychoanalytic Society, 1987.

Paskauskas, R. Andrew, ed. *The Complete Correspondence of Sigmund Freud and Ernest Jones, 1908–1939*. Cambridge: Harvard University Press, 1993.

Pettigrew, Eileen. *The Silent Enemy: Canada and the Deadly Flu of 1918*. Saskatoon: Western Producer Prairie Books, 1983.

Pickens, Donald K. *Eugenics and the Progressives*. Nashville: Vanderbilt University Press, 1968.

Porter, Roy. *A Social History of Madness: The World Through the Eyes of the Insane*. London: Weidenfeld & Nicholson, 1987.

———. *The Faber Book of Madness*. London: Faber & Faber, 1991.

Raymond, Jocelyn Moyter. *The Nursery World of Dr. Blatz*. Toronto: University of Toronto Press, 1991.

Real, Terrence. *I Don't Want to Talk About It: Overcoming the Secret Legacy of Male Depression*. New York: Scribner, 1997.

Reaume, Geoffrey. *Remembrance of Patients Past: Patient Life at the Toronto Hospital for the Insane, 1870–1940.* New York: Oxford University Press, 2000.

Roazen, Paul. *Freud and His Followers.* New York: Alfred A. Knopf, 1971.

Roland, Charles G. *Clarence Hincks: Mental Health Crusader.* Toronto: The Dundurn Group, 1989.

Roustang, François. *Dire Mastery: Discipleship From Freud to Lacan.* Paris: Les Éditions de Minuit, 1976.

Schwartz, Joseph. *Cassandra's Daughter: A History of Psychoanalysis.* London: Penguin Group UK, 1999.

Scull, Andrew. *Madhouse: A Tragic Tale of Megalomania and Modern Medicine.* New Haven: Yale University Press, 2005.

Shorter, Edward. *TPH: History and Memories of the Toronto Psychiatric Hospital, 1925–1966.* Toronto: Wall & Emerson, 1996.

————. *A History of Psychiatry: From the Era of the Asylum to the Age of Prozac.* 2nd ed. Hoboken: John Wiley & Sons, Inc., 1997.

Shortt, Samuel E.D., ed. *Medicine in Canadian Society: Historical Perspectives.* Montreal: McGill-Queen's University Press, 1981.

Showalter, Elaine. *The Female Malady: Women, Madness and English Culture, 1830–1980.* New York: Pantheon Books, 1985.

Stevenson, Lloyd. *Sir Frederick Banting.* Toronto: Ryerson Press, 1946.

Szasz, Thomas. *Coercion As Cure: A Critical History of Psychiatry.* Edison (NJ): Transaction Publishers, 2007.

Taylor, Kendall. *Sometimes Madness Is Wisdom: Zelda and Scott Fitzgerald, A Marriage.* New York: Ballantine, 2003.

Tracey, Patrick. *Stalking Irish Madness: Searching for the Roots of My Family's Schizophrenia.* New York: Bantam Books, 2008.

Turnbull, Andrew. *Scott Fitzgerald.* London: The Bodly Head Ltd., 1962.

Warsh, Cheryl Krasnick. *Moments of Unreason: The Practice of Canadian Psychiatry and the Homewood Retreat, 1833–1923.* Montreal: McGill-Queen's University Press, 1987.

Wear, Andrew, Ed. *Medicine In Society: Historical Essays.* New York: Cambridge University Press, 1992.

Whitaker, Robert. *Mad In America: Bad Science, Bad Medicine, and the Enduring Mistreatment of the Mentally Ill.* New York: Basic Books, 2002.

Wilson, David. *The Irish In Canada.* 2 vols. Ottawa: Canadian Historical Association, 1989.

Wrenshall, G. A., G. Hetenyi, Jr., and W. R. Feasby. *The Story of Insulin: 40 Years of Success Against Diabetes.* Bloomington: Indiana University Press, 1962.

ARTICLES:

Barreto, Luis, and Christopher J. Rutty. "The Speckled Monster: Canada, Smallpox and Its Eradication." *Canadian Journal of Public Health*, 93, no. 4 (August 2002): Special insert.

Bates, Gordon. "Lowering the Cost of Life-Saving: How the University of Toronto Is Performing Active Public Service." *Maclean's*, August 1915.

Bator, Paul. "Saving Lives on the Wholesale Plan: Public Health Reform in the City of Toronto, 1900–1930." PhD thesis, University of Toronto, 1979.

Brown, Thomas E. "Living with God's Afflicted: A History of the Provincial Lunatic Asylum at Toronto, 1830–1911." PhD thesis, Queen's University, 1980.

Callwood, June. "The Miracle Factory That Began In a Stable." *Maclean's*, October 1955.

Cameron, Donald. "The First Donald Fraser Memorial Lecture." *Canadian Journal of Public Health*, 51, no. 9 (September 1960): 341–348.

Connor, J.T.H. and Felicity Pope. "A Shocking Business: The Technology and Practice of Electrotherapeutics in Canada, 1840s to 1940s." *Material History Review* 49 (Spring 1999): 60–70.

Connaught Laboratories. *Annual Reports: 1914–1972.*

Defries, Craig. "Now Is the Time: The Early Years of Dr.

Robert Defries." master's thesis, Carleton University. 1993.

Defries, Robert. "Thirty-Five Years: The Connaught Medical Research Laboratories." *Canadian Journal of Public Health* 39, no. 8 (August 1948): 330–344.

Dolman, Claude. "Landmarks and Pioneers in the Control of Diphtheria." *Canadian Journal of Public Health* 64, no. 4 (August 1973): 317–336.

Dowbiggin, Ian. "C K. Clarke" in *Dictionary of Canadian Biography*, edited by Ramsay Cook et al, 15 (2005): 212–215.

Dubin, Martin David. "The League of Nations and the Development of the Public Health Profession." presentation, annual conference of the British International Studies Association, University of Warwick (December, 1991).

Edwards, Frederick. "A Peacetime Munitions Plant: Where Science Fashions Its Weapons Against the Armies of Disease." *Maclean's*, January 1928.

Farrar, Clarence B. "Psychiatry in Canada" (unpublished manuscript, CAMH Archives, 1952).

Farrar, Clarence B. "I Remember J. G. FitzGerald." *The American Journal of Psychiatry*, 120, no. 1 (July 1963): 49–52.

Fedunkiw, Marianne. "German Methods, Unconditional Gifts, and the Full-Time System: The Case Study of the University of Toronto, 1919–1923." *Canadian Bulletin of Medical History*, 21, no. 1 (January–June 2004): 5–39

Glasser, Ronald J. "We Are Not Immune: Influenza, SARS, and the Collapse of Public Health." *Harper's*, July 2004.

Godfrey, Charles. "C. K. Clarke: Biographical Essay." (unpublished manuscript, CAMH Archives. 1960s).

Greenland, Cyril. "Charles K. Clarke: A Pioneer of Canadian Psychiatry." Toronto: Clarke Institute of Psychiatry, 1966; 32 pp.

Greenland, Cyril. "Ernest Jones in Toronto, 1908–1913, Part I." *Canadian Psychiatric Association Journal*, 6, no. 3 (June 1961): 132–138.

Greenland, Cyril. "Ernest Jones in Toronto, 1908–1913, Part II."

Canadian Psychiatric Association Journal, 11, no. 6 (December 1966): 512–519.

Greenland, Cyril. "Ernest Jones in Toronto, 1908–1913, Part III." *Canadian Psychiatric Association Journal*, 12, no. 1 (February 1967): 79–81.

Greenland, Cyril. "Three Pioneers in Canadian Psychiatry." *JAMA*, 200, no. 1, (June 1967): 833–842.

Griffin, John D. and Cyril Greenland. "Treating the Mentally Ill in Ontario: A Documentary History of the Development of Mental Health Services in Ontario from 1867–1914" (unpublished manuscript, CAMH Archives, 1979).

Griffin, John D. "The Amazing Careers of Hincks and Beers." *Canadian Journal of Psychiatry*, 27, no. 8 (December 1982): 668–671.

Hopwood, Catherine. "Canadians and Psychoanalysis: The Early Years." graduate paper, department of sociology, McMaster University, 1991.

Johnston, Penelope. "Dr. C.K. Clarke: Fifty Years of Service to the Mentally Ill." *Medical Post*, December 1996.

Kindquist, Cathy. "Migration and Madness on the Upper Canadian Frontier, 1841–1850." The Canadian Papers in Rural History, 8, University of Guelph, 1992.

Lamb, Susan. "Nothing Human He Dare Ignore: Approaches to Psychiatry at the University of Toronto, 1927–1967." paper, department of history, University of Toronto, 2003.

Lewis, Jane. "The Prevention of Diphtheria in Canada and Britain, 1914–1945," *Journal of Social History*, 20 (1986): 163–176.

McConnachie, Kathleen. "Science and Ideology: The Mental Hygiene and Eugenics Movement in the Inter-War Years, 1919–1939." PhD thesis, University of Toronto, 1987.

Museum of Mental Health Services (Toronto). "The City and the Asylum." exhibition notes (1993).

Nicolson, Murray. "The Other Toronto: Irish Catholics in a Victorian City, 1850–1900," *Multicultural History Society of*

Ontario, 1984.

Pos, Robert, et al. "D. Campbell Myers, 1863–1927: Pioneer of Canadian General Hospital Psychiatry." *Canadian Psychiatric Association Journal,* 20, no. 5 (1975): 393–403.

Price, Gifford C. "A History of the Ontario Hospital, 1850–1950." master's thesis, University of Toronto, 1950.

Rutty, Christopher J. "'Do Something! . . . Do Anything!' Poliomyelitis in Canada, 1927–1962." PhD thesis, University of Toronto, 1995.

Rutty, Christopher J. "Robert Davies Defries, 1889–1975." In *Doctors, Nurses and Practitioners,* edited by L. N. Magner, 62–69. Westport, Conn.: Greenwood Press, 1997.

Rutty, Christopher J. "Personality, Politics and Canadian Health: The Origins of Connaught Medical Research Laboratories, University of Toronto, 1888–1917." In *Figuring the Social: Essays In Honour of Michael Bliss,* edited by E.A. Heaman, Alison Li, and Shelley McKellar, 273–303. Toronto: University of Toronto, 2008.

Rutty, Christopher J. "'Couldn't Live Without It': Diabetes, the Costs of Innovation, and the Price of Insulin in Canada, 1922–1984." *Canadian Bulletin of Medical History,* 25, no. 2, (2008), 407–431.

Seeman, Mary. "Psychiatry in the Nazi Era." *Canadian Journal of Psychiatry,* 50, no. 4 (March 2005).

Smith, Clifford. "Memories of the Connaught Laboratories: 1926–1969," unpublished manuscript, Sanofi Pasteur Archives (1983).

Wherrett, John. "A History of Neurology in Toronto, 1892–1960, Part I" *The Canadian Journal of Neurological Sciences,* 22, no. 4, (November 1995): 322–332.

Wherrett, John. "A History of Neurology in Toronto, 1892–1960, Part II" *The Canadian Journal of Neurological Sciences,* 23, no. 1, (February 1996): 63–75.

BROADCASTS AND TAPED INTERVIEWS:

O'Connell, Mary, producer. "Keeping This Young Country
     Sane." Radio broadcast, *Ideas*, CBC, October 13–14, 1999.

Clarence Hincks interviewed by Cyril Greenland, December
     1959, CAMH Archives.

Gordon Bates interviewed by Cyril Greenland and Jack Griffin,
     December 1965, CAMH Archives.

Neil McKinnon interviewed by Valerie Schatzker, July 1981,
     University of Toronto Archives.

INDEX

Page numbers in italics refer to material featured in photographs and their corresponding captions.

JAMES FitzGERALD is a journalist and author whose first book, *Old Boys: The Powerful Legacy of Upper Canada College*, was a controversial inside look at the attitudes and mores of Canada's ruling class. Revelations of the sexual abuse of boys at the school, first published in the book, led to the charging and conviction of three former teachers and the launching of a class action lawsuit against the college in 2002. The article that sparked *What Disturbs Our Blood* won a National Magazine Award. James lives in Toronto.